Whether this is the first time you've seen a copy of A Year with **Yours**, or if you're a loyal reader I can safely say you're in for a treat!

This unique miscellany is packed full of features to keep you entertained and inspired throughout the year ahead.

We've got practical advice to help you stay healthy, plus money-saving tips and household hints. There's plenty to read, too, with touching personal memories, evocative nostalgic photographs and exclusive short stories.

And if you're looking for inspiration, we've got ideas for days out, suggestions for hobbies and pastimes, 12 pretty and practical craft projects and a new recipe to try every week of the year.

This book is created with the help of **Yours** readers – it's their stories that make it so special – so, sincere thanks to all who contributed, including those whose letters we didn't have room to publish.

Happy reading – and best wishes for 2014

Sharon

Sharon Reid
Deputy and Specials Editor, **Yours** Magazine

Published by Pedigree in association with **Yours**
Pedigree Books Limited, Beech House, Walnut Gardens, Exeter, Devon EX4 4DH

Yours – the read of your life every fortnight! Look out for it in your local newsagent.
Yours, Bauer London Lifestyle, Media House, Peterborough Business Park, Peterborough PE2 6EA.
Tel: 01733 468000

Compiled and edited by Sharon Reid
Designed by David Reid
Sub-edited by Christine Curtis
Additional writing by Marion Clarke, Michelle Nightingale, Alex Frisby, Laura Bradder and Martine Gallie
Story illustrations by Kate Burgess

◆ All telephone numbers, website details and dates correct at time of going to press

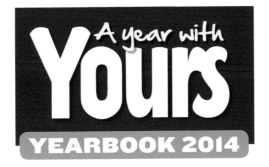

Name
Address
Postcode
Home phone
Mobile phone
Email

In case of emergency, contact:

Name
Telephone

Useful contacts

Bank	
Building society	
Chemist/pharmacy	
Chiropodist	
Council	
Credit card emergency	
Dentist	
Doctor	
Electrician	
Garage	
Hairdresser	
Hospital	
Local police	
Milkman	
Optician	
Plumber	
Solicitor	
Taxi	
Vet	

Renewal reminders

	Renewal date	Policy number	Telephone
Car insurance			
Car tax			
MOT			
Home insurance			
TV licence			
Pet insurance			
Yours subscription			

THE YEAR AHEAD

Stay healthy all year

Our up-to-the-minute health advice will help you stay fit and healthy whatever the season

January: reclaim your waist

Losing weight should be simple – eat less and be more active. Funny how it seems more difficult in real life, isn't it?

One thing is certain, crash diets are not the answer. They could harm your health and you are more likely to pile the weight back on afterwards. Making simple changes to your daily diet is a much better idea – here are few switches you can make today.

TOP TIP
Take advantage of longer nights to get some extra sleep – sleeping for at least six hours a night can help you to lose weight

Do a snack swap
We all need snacks to keep our energy levels up. The problem is that most of the snacks we eat – biscuits, cakes, crisps and chocolate – are high in sugar, fat and calories.

Next time your tummy rumbles reach for a piece of fruit, fruit bun, slice of malt loaf with low-fat spread or a small handful of almonds instead.

Switch to low–fat dairy
Dairy foods are an important part of our diet, but they can also harbour lots of fat and calories. Changing to semi-skimmed milk instead of full-cream and reduced-fat yogurts, cheese and cream is a fairly painless way to ditch a few calories.

Drink smart
We get a lot of our extra calories from fizzy drinks and fruit juice. Put a jug of water on the table at mealtimes instead, and add a little water to fruit juice. Plus, of course, keep an eye on how much calorie-laden alcohol you drink – one glass of wine contains 136 calories.

Make your own takeaway
If you love a takeaway, try making your own healthier versions at home.

Turn a cheap cut of lamb into a tasty shish kebab or make your own pizza using a shop-bought base and reduced-calorie mozzarella.

round

February: boost your mood

It's easy to feel down in the dumps at this time of the year. These simple pick-me-ups will help to cheer you up until spring.

Stay active
Exercise not only helps to boost your energy levels and immune system, but also causes your brain to release endorphins – naturally occurring chemicals that make you feel happier.

Get the T factor
The amino acid tryptophan is vital for the manufacture of the feelgood hormone serotonin in our bodies, and also helps to promote good sleep. Tryptophan is found in a variety of protein-rich foods, including soya, red meat, chicken, turkey, fish, eggs, nuts, seeds, cheddar cheese and milk.

Eat well
Stock up on oily fish, which is rich in omega-3 fatty acids, to help block chemicals that cause low mood. Fruit, vegetables and wholegrain are good for balancing blood sugar and keep your energy levels stable.

See a friend
Even if you don't feel like it, make an effort to see friends and family. Face-to-face human contact prompts physiological responses in your brain that boost your mental health.

Try St John's Wort
This popular herbal remedy is an effective treatment for mild to moderate depression. Do speak to your GP or pharmacist if you are thinking of trying it though, as it can interact with other drugs and it can have side effects.

Be mindful
Mindfulness is a combination of meditation, yoga and breathing techniques, which has been proven to help ease depression. All the techniques are designed to help you focus on the present rather that dwelling on the past or worrying about the present. **Find out more at www.bemindful.co.uk.**

March: bump up energy levels

One in five of us report feeling tired all the time. Hormones, poor sleep and conditions such as arthritis can all contribute. Try these simple energisers…

Stop stress
Stress uses up a lot of energy. Try to introduce relaxing activities into every day – a walk with the dog, listening to music, reading or spending time with friends could all improve your energy.

Cut sugar and caffeine
Sugar doesn't boost your energy, it steals it. Try putting a smaller spoon in your sugar bowl!

Most of us reach for a cup of tea or coffee when we're flagging, but you may actually find your energy levels are better if you reduce the amount of caffeine you are having. Try cutting down over three weeks to see if your energy levels improve.

Drink more water
Sometimes we feel tired when, actually, we're dehydrated. Next time you need a lift, drink a glass of water and see if you notice the difference.

Sleep better
Experts recommend getting up at the same time every morning if you are having problems sleeping, and only going to bed when you feel tired. If you are wakeful during the night, go to another room and do something relaxing until you feel sleepy again.

Get plenty of iron
Too little iron in your diet can leave you feeling fatigued. Good sources of iron include lean red meat, chicken (the dark meat is best), oily fish like sardines, green leafy vegetables, baked beans and fortified breakfast cereals. ➡

April: 5 steps to stronger bones

It's never too late to improve your bone health and protect yourself from osteoporosis – just follow our five easy steps.

1 Stay active
Weight-bearing exercise is best for your bones – that's exercise in which you support the weight of your own body. Try jogging, aerobics, tennis, dancing, vacuuming or even brisk walking.

2 Bump up your calcium
Calcium-rich foods provide the vitamins and minerals you need for strong bones. Milk and other dairy products, including the low-fat varieties are excellent sources, but you can also find calcium in a range of other foods, including green leafy vegetables, dried fruit, tinned fish (with bones) and tofu.

3 Get some sunshine
Sunshine is the best source of Vitamin D, which your body needs to absorb calcium. Ten minutes of sun exposure daily on your bare arms and face between May and September will help make sure you're getting enough. If you are over 65, you should also take a supplement – speak to your GP.

4 Clean up your lifestyle
Smoking and excessive alcohol are bad for bones, as both can speed up the rate at which bones thin. Women should drink no more than two units a day (one large glass of wine).

5 Find your ideal weight
Carrying a bit of weight can actually be good for your bones – being underweight is a known risk factor for osteoporosis. But too much excess fat can actually weaken bones.

May: Happy, healthy feet

Dreading the thought of getting your feet into summer sandals now the weather is warmer? We answer your queries about some common foot problems.

Q How do I relieve the pain of bunions?

A Bunion pads worn over the painful joints will help ease pressure and prevent your shoes rubbing. They are available from chemists and pharmacies. Night splints and even exercises can help, but speak to a chiropodist first. To find a chiropodist near you call 0207 234 8620 or visit www.scpod.org.

Q My heels are cracked – what can I do?

A Scrub your heels daily with a nailbrush to keep them clean and prevent a build up of dirt forming and making cracks and calluses deeper. Then apply a heel cream, ideally with at least 10 per cent urea content. Once a week use a foot file or pumice stone to gently remove hard areas. Avoid using the metal cheese grater type of file as they can inflame and aggravate the skin.

Q My toenails are thick and yellow – what could it be?

A If you notice your toenails becoming thick, yellow and crumbly it's likely to be a fungal nail infection. There is a range of treatments for fungal infections available from your pharmacist if your infection is in the early stages. If it's serious, you may need to visit your doctor for an oral treatment called Terbinafine. You may need a blood test to check your liver function before this is prescribed

Q Why is the skin between my toes itchy and sore?

A Itchy flaky skin between your toes is likely to be caused by the fungal infection athlete's foot. This thrives in dark, damp places so shoes make the perfect breeding ground. As a preventative measure wash and air your feet regularly, wear cotton socks and make sure you air shoes thoroughly. To banish it apply surgical spirit between your toes daily to help dry the area out or use an over-the-counter athlete's foot treatment.

TOP TIP
Treat swollen feet to a soak in warm water then try making a 'fist' with your feet for ten seconds, then release and repeat.

June: Get active

Summer's finally here and it's time to get some fresh air and enjoy the great outdoors. If you're not quite sure where to begin, here are a few ideas to get you started.

Start walking

Brisk walking is a good example of a moderate intensity activity that gives your heart the workout it needs. Try jotting down how many minutes of walking you do each day. You could start by walking for five minutes three times a day on three days a week. Walk at a slightly faster pace than usual, without it being uncomfortable. See if you can build up to 30 minutes on at least five days a week.

Do some gardening

Mowing and raking the lawn counts towards your 150 minutes a week of moderate intensity physical activity. Lifting pots, carrying and digging will also help to strengthen your muscles, while stretching and reaching as you work helps keep your joints supple. Being out in the fresh air will help you de-stress and boost your mood, too.

Try a free outdoor gym

Check to see if your local park has a 'trim trail'. This is an outdoor area with pieces of exercise equipment that you can use for free. You could also contact your local council to ask whether there's one near you or type 'trim trail' and your area into your internet search engine. Perhaps see if you can persuade a friend to go along with you as well.

Have fun with the grandchildren

Little ones don't need any encouragement to get out into the fresh air. Why not borrow your grandchildren for an afternoon and head for your local park with some bats and balls, hula hoops and a picnic. Look out for reasonably priced children's outdoor activity packs in your local supermarket. ➡

July: Enjoy the sun – safely

We sort the myths from the facts about sun safety, so you can make the most of the summertime without putting your health at risk.

FACT! We need sunlight to get enough Vitamin D

Some sun exposure is essential for keeping us healthy because it's our main source of Vitamin D, which is important for building and maintaining strong bones. However, too much is the main cause of skin cancer, so when it comes to sun exposure, little and often is best. A matter of a few minutes at midday without sunscreen on sunny days should be enough.

MYTH! You don't need sunscreen in this country

Most cases of sunburn happen at home rather than abroad. Getting sunburned once every two years can triple your risk of melanoma, the most serious form of skin cancer. Remember, sunburn can just as easily happen when you're out and about rather than deliberately sunbathing.

MYTH! Any old sunscreen will do

It's vital to apply at least a SPF15 broad-spectrum sunscreen with a star rating of four or five stars. Use at least two tablespoons to cover your whole body if wearing a swimming costume and don't be tempted to dust off those bottles you've been hoarding in your bathroom cabinet, as most only last two to three years.

Be mole aware

Get to know your moles – spotting the early warning signs of melanoma increases your chance of successful treatment. If you notice a change in the size, shape or colour of a mole or patch of skin, visit your GP to have it checked – even if you don't think it's anything to worry about.

FACT! Anyone can develop skin cancer

We should all be taking precautions to safeguard our health for the future but it's true some of us are at higher risk than others. If you're fair-skinned, have lots of moles, a personal history of sunburn or a family history of skin cancer you're more at risk and need to take extra care to protect your skin.

August: Natural cures for summer ailments

Summer health niggles needn't mean a trip to the GP or chemist. Here are a few simple natural remedies you can try at home.

Heat rash

Avoid anything that is going to make your feel warmer, including hot drinks, alcohol and synthetic clothing. Have a tepid bath with about 6tsp baking soda added or, alternatively, bathe the area with cooled mint tea, which has a wonderfully cooling effect. Aloe vera gel is another ideal soother for summer rashes – keep a tube in your fridge.

Insect stings

For bee and wasp stings, add a drop of neat geranium, oregano, tea tree or thyme oil. (With bee stings you will need to remove the sting first by scraping it off with your fingernail or the blunt side of a knife.) Then put a cold, damp flannel on top to soothe the pain.

Hayfever

To relieve irritated nasal passages, aromatherapist, Daniele Ryman, suggests you boil some eucalyptus leaves in a pan of water, then drain. Put the liquid into an ironing spray bottle and spray your bedroom before you go to bed. For itchy eyes, put two chamomile teabags into some warm water for a minute or two. Squeeze them out, then lie down and rest them on your eyes for about 10 minutes.

Nettle stings

Nettle stings are caused by an acidic irritant. To soothe the pain, mix alkaline baking soda with water to form a paste and cover the affected area.

Sunburn

Add two drops of lavender essential oil to 3tbsp plain yoghurt straight from the fridge. Mix well and apply to burned skin.

September: 8 easy ways to live longer

You don't have to overhaul your lifestyle completely to live a long and healthy life. You can add a few years to your lifespan by making a few simple changes today.

1 Smile!
Research shows that smiling doesn't just show that you're happy, it actually makes you happier too.

2 Get your blood pressure checked
Age UK estimates that five million of us have raised blood pressure without knowing it. Although you can't tell if your blood pressure is high, your GP can check it in just a couple of minutes.

3 Be grateful
Research shows that grateful people tend to be happy people. Once a day bring to mind ten things that you are grateful for, counting them on your fingers.

4 Buy some fish
Only 28 per cent of us eat the recommended two portions of fish a week. Smoked, tinned, frozen or fresh, fish is an important part of a healthy, varied diet.

5 Cook a meal
It's easy not to bother with proper meals, especially if you live on your own, but there is evidence that those of us who make regular use of our cookers enjoy longer lives.

6 Floss your teeth
Bacteria associated with unhealthy gums have been shown to increase our risk of a range of serious health problems including heart disease and stroke.

7 Have one extra vegetable
Packed with vitamins, antioxidants and fibre, vegetables protect against lots of serious conditions, such as cancer or heart disease, so aim for at least one extra portion every day.

8 Write down what you eat
Why diet when you can control your weight simply by noting down what you eat each day? In a year-long study, female dieters who kept daily food journals lost about 6lb (2.7kg) more than those who didn't. ➡

October: Bump up your brainpower

We've all heard the phrase 'use it or lose it' but it's true that an active mind is a healthy mind. Crosswords, quizzes, chess games, learning to play an instrument, singing and even travelling abroad have all been shown to boost brain power. Keeping your brain active is what counts – so switch on the TV and challenge yourself to learn something new.

Having high blood pressure also ups your risk of memory problems, say American scientists. If you don't exercise, are overweight, smoke, eat a lot of salt or fat, are under a lot of stress, or just haven't had your blood pressure checked in a while, see you GP for a check-up.

Maintaining a healthy weight is important too, because it lowers your risk of high blood pressure, stroke and heart disease, all of which have an impact on the likelihood of developing memory problems. So, shedding a few pounds won't just help you to slip back into your favourite trousers, it could help to improve you memory and concentration.

Or why not grab your walking shoes? Researchers have found that regular exercise could help keep your brain sharp. People who walked for 40 minutes three times a week for a year saw significant improvement in their memories. Scientists believe that aerobic exercise such as walking, dancing or playing tennis helps to get extra oxygen to your brain, which keeps it healthy.

A good night's sleep is vital too – and not just because it gives

TOP TIP
If you struggle to remember names or lists, try setting them to a catchy tune. Research shows it makes them easier to remember.

your body time to carry out vital repairs. US psychologists have also discovered that people who think things over before bed and then sleep on their thoughts are much better at putting their plans into action the following day.

November: Beat those winter bugs

The cold season is here and the last thing any of us want is to be stuck in bed with a box of tissues. Our tried-and-tested tips will bolster your immune system and help you avoid nasty winter bugs.

Probiotic protection
Our digestive systems are an important part of our immune defences. Probiotic or 'good' bacteria can help to maintain gut health by keeping levels of harmful bacteria down. Probiotic bacteria are often added to yoghurts and yoghurt drinks – look out for them in the supermarket.

Sleep like a baby
Enjoying a good night's sleep won't just leave you feeling refreshed. Good-quality sleep also helps to keep your immune system strong and protects you against coughs, colds and more serious diseases such as type 2 diabetes. Scientists aren't sure why this is. However, they do know that levels of disease-fighting cells called T-cells tend to drop in sleep-deprived people.

Cut down stress
While a little stress helps to keep us on our toes, too much can weaken our immune systems. Scientists in the US recently asked people how stressful the last 12 months had been before putting drops containing a cold virus in their nose. The people who had been most stressed were twice as likely to catch a cold. Learn to recognise the signs of stress, such as tense, tired muscles

Did you know?
Have you heard the one about...? Laughter reduces the level of stress hormones in our bodies and increases the amount of infection-fighting antibodies.

or irritability and use them as a signal to take it easy for a while.

Get your vitamins
To get a good range of nutrients, make sure you are eating lots of colourful fruit and vegetables, such as peas, sweetcorn, carrots, sweet potatoes, red peppers, broccoli, cabbage, red grapes and kiwi fruit. The mineral zinc helps to keep your immune system strong too, and can help to fight off colds. Good sources include chicken, beef, dairy products and wholegrain foods.

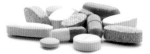

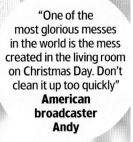

"One of the most glorious messes in the world is the mess created in the living room on Christmas Day. Don't clean it up too quickly"
American broadcaster Andy

December: Have a calm Christmas

With presents to buy, meals to cook and visitors to entertain, Christmas can be a stressful, as well as a pleasurable, time of year. We'll help you keep your cool throughout the festive season.

Write a worry list

You've already written a Christmas card list and a present list, so spend a few minutes writing a list of your worries. What are you most dreading? Who, or what, could help? Is there someone you can confide in? The sooner you face your biggest concerns, the easier they'll be to manage.

It doesn't have to be homemade

Last year you may have made your own apricot and walnut stuffing. If you decide to take an easier route this year, so what? Wouldn't you rather watch your family open their presents than be stirring the gravy?

Invite a new guest

If family tension is your main concern, change the dynamic by inviting someone new. A different face around the table, especially someone who might otherwise have been alone, is a great way to bring out the best in everyone.

Try aromatherapy

Essential oils like lavender, sandalwood and clary sage are excellent stress relievers. Add a few drops to your bath or put them in a mug of boiling water, position your head about 12 inches away, and slowly inhale.

It's good to say no

Is your family treating you like their own personal shopper? Stop saying 'yes' to everything they ask. Perhaps, you're the one making heavy demands of yourself? Banish the words 'should' and 'must' from your vocabulary and see what a difference it makes.

Keep drinking

Er… no, not alcohol – that only dehydrates you and makes your liver work overtime to process it. Instead, develop a healthy drink habit by drinking lots of water, which hydrates every part of the body and helps you cope better with stressful situations.

7 of the best days

1 'New-Look' Stonehenge

Amesbury, Wiltshire, SP4 7DE
Hopefully the weather will be good enough for you to be able to enjoy Stonehenge now it's been re-developed… or do we mean 'un-developed'? Not only do the changes mean an improved site with better parking, but there's more green space. With the A344 removed, there's simply miles of space, with travel provided to and from the Visitors' Centre. We say it's a change for the better. Entry is free to English Heritage and National Trust members.
Call 0870 333 1181 or visit stonehengevisitorcentre.org

2 Sharnfold Farm

Stone Cross, E Sussex, BN24 5BU
At Stone Cross, just a stone's throw from the coast, is Sharnfold Farm and Shop. Spring sees Farmer Dennis feeding the lambs; ideal for getting little ones involved in the fun. There's a farm trail that passes the fishing lakes, where you can view all the different flora and fauna as it bursts into life. From April, you can pick your own rhubarb, and there will be local asparagus in the Farm shop. With free parking and an excellent coffee shop, Sharnfold is an ideal spring destination, whatever the weather.
Call 01323 768490 or visit www.sharnfoldfarm.co.uk

3 The Eden Project

Bodelva, Cornwall, PL24 2SG
Need reminding what green looks like? Sometimes spring needs a little helping hand and that's where the Eden Project comes in. Bringing the outdoors indoors, Eden showcases all things gardening and horticultural. It also contributes to charity and community projects, and has already raised over £1 billion for the local economy. Get involved – there are gardening courses to flex your green fingers, or a quick visit to the rainforest to perk you up for the day. Be sure to try the treetop lookout if you can!
Call 01726 811911 or visit www.edenproject.com

4 Knowsley Estate

Prescot, Merseyside, L34 4AG
Our spring pick for a day when you don't know what the weather's doing! On one hand there's the drive-through Safari, perfect for being outside without risking getting wet. Don't want to drive? Hop on the Baboon Bus! On the other hand, there's the Chill Out Spa – arrive along the tree-lined driveway and truly relax in this secluded location, with 2,500 acres of parkland between you and the world.
Call 01514 894827 or visit www.knowsley.com for further details about what's available throughout the estate.

5 RHS Show Cardiff

Cardiff Castle, Castle Street, CF10 3RB
At the height of spring, the RHS fills Cardiff Castle with life. Every April, the show celebrates the best of Welsh gardening and produce in one of the country's finest locations. Springtime attracts visitors seeking new ideas for the gardening year ahead, and as the first major show of the year, Cardiff is a great place to start. With plenty of plants and other gardening items on sale, there's something for everyone to take home. Run in partnership with Cardiff Council, the show is known for being intimate and friendly.
For tickets, call 0844 871 7677 or visit www.rhs.org.uk/Shows

out... for spring!

PIC RHS

6 Daffodils at Sizergh Castle

nr. Kendal, Cumbria, LA8 8AE
Come and see the inspiration for Wordsworth's famous poem: wild daffodils in all their glory, at the gateway to the Lake District. Also in spring, see tulips on the top terrace, cherry blossom in the Dutch garden and seasonal colour in the limestone rock garden. Indoors is wood panelling, once displayed in the Victoria and Albert museum, now back in its original location.

It's a good day out, and a great stopping place 'en-route', just five miles from junction 36 of the M6. Free entry to National Trust members.
Call 01539 560951 or visit www.nationaltrust.org.uk/sizergh

7 Padstow May Day

Padstow, Cornwall, PL28 8AF
May 1 is Padstow's "Obby 'Oss Day'. The small town becomes packed with many thousands of people who watch the wearer of the 'Obby 'Oss (Hobby

Horse) costume dance through the streets, accompanied by musicians and drummers. The folklore behind it is widely debated, but go along to sing the traditional May Day song with the Padstonians, and you might understand what all the fuss is about. Be advised that the area can get very crowded and may not be suitable for wheelchairs or those with mobility issues.
For further information call 01841 533449 or visit www.padstowlive.com.

7 of the best days

1 The Royal Edinburgh Military Tattoo

Edinburgh Castle, EH1 2NG

Here's one tattoo that isn't at all painful! For amazing live pipe, drum and band music head to magical Edinburgh Castle. Enjoy the best of Scottish as well as performances from overseas. The 2014 Tattoo runs from August 1-23. It's set quite high up with slopes and cobbles, which could be tricky if you have difficulties walking. Wheelchair users must be accompanied by an able-bodied person; however, if this is the case that person may enter for free.

To find out more, call 0131 225 1188 or visit www.edintattoo.co.uk

2 Port Eliot Festival

St. Germans, Saltash, Cornwall, PL12 5ND

Make a note in your diary to get down to St. Germans for July 24-27. Port Eliot celebrates publishing, music and the visual arts, but most important is its dedication to fun. Some 'wordy' festivals can feel a bit stuffy but Port Eliot wants to put its visitors at ease. We recommend the open-air Paradiso Cinema (a nice play on words of a favourite film of ours!) Not only are the films top notch, but the backdrop is none other than Isambard Kingdom Brunel's railway viaduct.

For more, call 01503 232783 or visit www.porteliotfestival.com

3 Ryde Carnival

Isle of Wight, PO33

August is festival month on the island, with floats and marching bands parading from town to village. Finally these arrive at Ryde, for the best performance of the season. Reputedly the oldest established carnival in England, the first true event was held in 1888 – but the original celebrated Queen Victoria's 1887 Diamond Jubilee. These days, while still keeping their distinct island character, the flamboyant dancers, creative floats and giant-costumed characters are more akin to Rio than Ryde – and it's all free!

For further information including starting times and routes, call Isle of Wight Tourism on 01983 813813 or visit www.rydecarnival.org.uk and www.iwight.com

4 Summer Roses at RHS

Garden Hyde Hall, Rettendon, Essex, CM3 8ET

For a beautiful bevvy of blooms, visit the Hilltop Garden at Hyde Hall. Admire the rope walk made from climbing roses and clematis, and the rolling hills with its swathes of grass. There's also the Dry Garden, with its Mediterranean influence, home to more than 400 species of drought-resistant plants – and that's why we're recommending Hyde for summer colour outdoors. It's your best bet in drier times. Open 10am-6pm, last entry one hour before closing. Each RHS member plus one guest enters for free.

For further information call 0845 265 8071 or visit www.rhs.org.uk/gardens/hyde–hall

5 Arundel Castle

West Sussex, BN18 9AB

Open for the summer season, 11th century Arundel Castle has lots to offer for a great day out. Take a guided tour, or explore the building at your leisure. Discover the Baron's Hall, Library, and Fitzalan Chapel before climbing the Norman Motte and Keep. In fine weather there's The Collector Earl's Garden to explore – and as part of the season's festivities, Shakespearian performances to watch. Easy access to the restaurant and coffee shop.

For further information about events and prices, call 01903 882173 or visit www.arundelcastle.org

out... for summer!

6 Geocaching with the National Trust

Various locations

An adventure with a difference! If you're after family fun or an afternoon outdoors honing your skills, try geocaching. It's modern orienteering – you pick up a GPS (Global Positioning System) device from your local participating National Trust centre, use it to follow 'digital clues' and discover treasure outdoors! You're looking for 'caches' – hidden, waterproof boxes that are out there waiting for you… if you can find them! Trails are set up so you can explore the local area while on your mission.

To find your nearest geocaching location, call the National Trust on 0844 800 1895 or visit www.nationaltrust.org.uk

7 History Live!

Kelmarsh Hall, Kelmarsh, Northamptonshire, NN6 9LY

This is English Heritage's flagship event, which takes place every summer. Re-enactors, interpreters and performers tell more than 2,000 years of English history. Enjoy a good old medieval joust from the shade of a tree that might just have witnessed a few hundred years of history! The event used to be known as the 'Festival of History' but Head of Events, Emily Burns, says: "We have changed the name to better reflect that the event is focused on visitors truly taking part."

For further information and to buy tickets, call 0870 333 1181 or visit www.historylive.com

7 of the best days

1 Last Invasion Tapestry

Town Hall, Fishguard, Pembrokeshire, SA65 9HE

Our pick of autumnal getaways is beautiful Pembrokeshire – there's still plenty open, to be enjoyed without the summer crowds. Free attractions include the Pentre Ifan burial chamber, high up in the Preseli Hills, and the Last Invasion Tapestry at Fishguard. This amazing, 30 metre tapestry tells the story of Britain's last mainland invasion – which took place in 1797. It was the French who tried to take Fishguard… they must have sailed quite a way!

For more about the tapestry, call Fishguard Town Hall on 01437 776636 or visit www.pembrokeshire.org.uk

2 Melton Mowbray Food Festival

The Cattle Market, LE13 1JY

Melton Mowbray plays host to this delicious date on the first weekend of October – this year, the 4th and 5th. The best East Midlands delicacies are on sale, along with samples and theatre demonstrations to keep you up-to-date on what's grown and what's great to eat in the area.

The site is fairly flat and hard standing so there's no need for wellies or worries about getting around. Just give your taste buds a treat! Plus the under 16s enter for free – so make it a family day out for less.

For more information, call 07944 204 555 or visit www.meltonmowbrayfoodfestival.co.uk

3 Deer Rutting Weekend

Selworthy, Exmoor National Park, Somerset, TA24 8TJ

A unique opportunity to see wild stags during the rutting season, accompanied by National Trust experts. This weekend programme includes learning about these majestic creatures as well as venturing out late afternoon and early morning, when the deer are most active and the light is at its best for taking photographs. You'll stay in Holnicote House and, in leisure time, you may want to visit nearby Minehead, Lynton or Lynmouth.

For further information and to book, contact HF Holidays – they're the UK's largest walking and leisure activity holiday organisation. Call 0845 470 8558 or visit www.hfholidays.co.uk

4 Autumn Steam Gala

North Yorkshire Moors Railway, Pickering, YO18 7AJ

This rather special heritage line runs between Pickering and Grosmont, and then on to Whitby. Come along for the 41st annual Autumn Steam Gala; a fantastic opportunity to see demonstrations, models, and locomotives on the line. Why not board and take a trip through the Moors in their autumnal glory? Along the way, stop at Goathland station – or rather, Aidensfield (the setting for popular TV programme Heartbeat). Younger visitors might even recognise it as Harry Potter's Hogsmeade… 2014's gala will almost certainly be taking place in late September.

For further information and to book, call 01751 472 508 or visit www.nymr.co.uk

out... **for autumn!**

5 Galloway Kite Trail

Bellymack Hill Farm, nr. Castle Douglas, Dumfries, DG7 2PJ
Combine an autumnal walk with the spectacular sight of kites soaring overhead. These impressive birds have wingspans almost as wide as we humans are tall. The RSPB are committed to preserving the habitat for kites; however you're also likely to glimpse kestrels, ospreys, and even a red squirrel or two. There's a small admission fee for adults to the feeding station, but children go free, so we recommend you visit around the 2pm feeding time – though the farm is open 12-4pm.
For further information call 01556 670464 or visit www.rspb.co.uk/datewithnature.

6 Creative Crafts Shows

Sandown Park, Surrey, KT10 9AJ and King's Hall, Belfast, BT9 6GW
Keep warm indoors at these Stitch and Creative Crafts Shows – not only are they a great day out, but they'll keep you busy for weeks to come. Find inspiration for your usual hobby or discover something completely new with these 'make and take' workshops, demonstrations and hundreds of supplies on sale. Whether you're the cross-stitch queen or a dab hand at beading, there's bound to be something that catches your eye here. The show comes to Surrey on Sept 4-6 and Belfast Nov 13-15.
For tickets and information call 01822 617 744 or visit www.sccshows.co.uk

7 Hops and Harvest Beer Festival

Kent Life, Maidstone, ME14 3AU
Autumn is the time for hop-picking, so head to Kent Life, where visitors get the chance to have a go at the time-honoured tradition of picking hops by hand at the Hops 'n' Harvest Beer Festival. Enjoy live music and the chance to sample up to 60 varieties of rare and not-so-rare real ales and ciders, see the last working coal-fired oast house in Britain, stroll around 28 acres of lovely grounds and gardens, and meet characters from Kent's past. This year it's scheduled for Sept 13-14.
For more information call 01622 763 936 or visit www.kentlife.org.uk

7 of the best days

1 Grey Seal Spotting

North Wirral foreshore and Hilbre Island, Merseyside, CH47
With the Irish Sea and Welsh hills in the distance, this estuary is home to stoical grey seals. Come and visit them and their entertaining neighbours! If you're in need of some fresh winter air, take a stroll along the Hoylake promenade (parking, toilets and optics for viewing are all nearby). You'll find RSPB-led events going on from Wednesdays to Sundays, including bracing walks over the sands to fantastic sights. Some events on the island will see you temporarily cut off by the tide, so waterproofs and flasks are advised!
Call 01513 538478 or visit www.rspb.co.uk/datewithnature

2 Medieval Christmas Market

Lincoln City Centre, LN1
This Christmas market might be old – really old – but it's still our favourite. The Park and Ride scheme makes it easy to get into this beautiful city of sloping rooftops and cobbled streets, and once you're here the one-way system helps to keep the crowd moving, so what you get is a bustling atmosphere without the usual struggling for position.
Enjoy mulled wine in the castle grounds, browse festive stalls with the cathedral as a backdrop, and keep warm and merry with the best-dressed and costumed folk.
Call 01522 873503 or visit lincoln-christmasmarket.co.uk

3 Burning the Clocks

Madeira Drive, Brighton, East Sussex, BN2 1PS
Celebrate the Winter Solstice with charity Same Sky. Each December 21st, thousands of people 'burn the clocks' – paper and willow lanterns to mark the shortest day of the year. Locals carry their lanterns through the city and arrive at the beach to fireworks and live music! It's a lovely alternative to bonfire night, thought up in the mid-nineties as a way for everyone to celebrate the festive season together, regardless of faith. Best of all, it's free, so why not get involved in something a bit different this year?
Call 01273 571106 or visit www.visitbrighton.com.

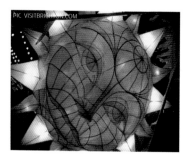

PIC VISITBRIGHTON.COM

4 The Winter Fair, Royal Welsh Showground

Llanelwedd, Powys, LD2 3SY
Combine some Christmas shopping with the best livestock event in the UK and what do you get? The Winter Fair, of course! From displays of cows, horses, sheep and more, through to local produce in the Food Hall and unusual festive gifts, it's a welcome addition to the Welsh annual calendar, kick-starting Advent each year. Wales' Craft Council also put in an appearance, and children under four enter for free. The 2014 fair is on from Dec 1-2.
For more information, call 01982 553683, to book call 0844 545 0517 or visit www.rwas.co.uk/winter-fair

out... for winter!

PIC: ELECTRIC EGG

5 Victorian Christmas at Audley End

Saffron Walden, Essex, CB11 4JF
Every year, Audley End celebrates the festive season in true Victorian style. From traditional decorations to 19th century storytelling and cooking, the place positively breathes charm and goodwill. It's because of Queen Victoria and Prince Albert that us Brits celebrate Christmas the way we do – so it seems a fitting tribute to experience the festivities in Victorian style. Discover what goes on 'below stairs', and meet a certain special someone who will be spreading his own particular cheer…
Tickets must be booked in advance, dates to follow. Call 0870 333 1183 to find out more or visit www.english-heritage.org.uk

6 Dunham Massey Winter Gardens

Altrincham, Cheshire, WA4 4SJ
Dunham Massey is the largest garden of its kind in the UK. Its seven acres are home to more than 700 different plant species and a further 1,600 shrubs, providing plenty of distraction from the cold. Head Gardener Damian Harris explains the changes it's been through since it opened in 2009: "Many of the shrubs, newly planted then, are now well established and the growing trees are adding structure and height. Flowering has increased and shrub stems have matured, providing even better colour."
Free entry to National Trust Members. For further information call 0161 941 1025 or visit www.nationaltrust.org.uk/dunham-massey

7 Festival of Winter Walks:

Various locations (England, Scotland and Wales)
Make the most of the daylight hours by taking part in the Ramblers popular Festival of Winter Walks, with hundreds of walks across Britain. From short, festive jaunts to heartier rambles, there'll be plenty on offer for you, your family and friends to enjoy. Chosen and led by Ramblers volunteers, the walks showcase Britain at its wintry best. There's an open invite to everyone, whatever their age or walking ability… so discover the benefits of being outdoors as you walk into the New Year with the Ramblers.
For details call the central office on 020 7339 8500 or visit www.ramblers.org.uk/winterwalks

Fill your free time

Searching for fresh ideas to keep you busy in retirement?
Look no further than our selection of popular pastimes

A — Aqua Aerobics

Exercising in water is great as you get older as it supports the body, putting less stress on your joints and muscles. Water pressure also helps the heart move blood around the body. Aqua aerobics classes are a fun way to get an all-over workout, and break the monotony of swimming lengths. Most local pools will offer these classes, and they should provide any equipment you might need.

B — Bird watching

If you're a nature lover, there's no better hobby than bird watching, as it gets you close to some wonderful creatures while also enjoying a fantastic outdoor walk. As early mornings are the best time to spot active and vocal birds, it also ensures you have a reason to drag yourself out of bed! Bird Watching magazine will give you a great guide to getting started, available from all good newsagents.

C — Calligraphy

A relaxing pastime, calligraphy is a great starting point for anyone wanting to discover their creative side, and it's as rewarding as it is enjoyable. Patience is required to learn the smooth strokes, but once you've mastered the basic letters, there are so many ways to use this skill, from writing Christmas cards to making decorative place names. Try it in the comfort of your own home, or find a calligraphy course at www.clas.co.uk for a more social experience.

D — Découpage

If you're after a simple craft, this could be for you. Découpage involves using old magazines, maps or decorative paper to embellish old objects such as boxes or small pieces of furniture. The pieces are cut out and glued on to the object, then coated with varnish until the joins are no longer visible, giving the illusion of paintwork. Projects and kits become more advanced as you progress with the hobby – visit your local craft shop to buy some basic tools.

E — Ebay

Many of us find ourselves downsizing and decluttering as we get older, but deciding what to do with the items can be tricky. If you're computer savvy, then auction site Ebay is a great way to make money from your unwanted items, and the more time you spend mastering the skill of selling, the better you'll become. Visit www.ebay.co.uk for a seller's guide. Be warned though – this hobby can become very addictive!

F – Film club

If you're a film buff, but are bored with the Hollywood blockbusters, there are plenty of opportunities to turn your interest into a regular hobby. Many towns and cities have film societies showing older or less mainstream films. These generally run in seasons, and are often held in local libraries or colleges. If you fancy something cosier, get a group of friends together to host DVD nights, and watch and discuss your chosen films over a glass of wine!

G – Grow your own

You don't have to have a large garden to make growing your own produce an enjoyable pastime. Herbs such as chives, thyme and tarragon can thrive in windowsill containers, as can tomato plants, providing they receive enough light and regular attention. For a more social aspect, why not join a community allotment – a green space cared for and maintained by groups of volunteers. Your local council should be able to point you in the right direction.

H – Hiking

Hiking sounds like a high-energy activity, but you can really tailor it to your personal fitness. It's a great exercise choice as it's free, low impact, and you can do it anywhere! You may be able to plan your own route in your local area, but if you fancy travelling further afield, then contact the Ramblers Association for trail ideas www.ramblers.org.uk, 020 7339 8500). Buy a good pair of hiking boots, then get out and see nature at its best. ➡

A - Z of Hobbies

I – IT classes

Getting started with a computer can be daunting, particularly if you don't have a more experienced friend or family member to hand. Before you splash out on a new laptop or iPad, it's worth nipping down to your local library and signing up to an IT class. They're usually free, and you'll be given one-on-one tuition to guide you through. Or if you're the technological wizard, then why not volunteer a spare hour or two to help lead a class?

J – Jewellery making

If you've got an interest in fashion, then this could be the craft for you – and it's perfect for saving money when it comes to presents too! Handmade jewellery always has sentimental value, and provides the wearer with something truly unique. If you get really good, you could always sell your creations too! Jewellery making kits are widely available from craft shops, but try a local haberdashery for more unusual beads and decorative pieces.

K – Knitting

It may sound like the oldest hobby in the book, but knitting is having a revival. It's reported that even celebrities such as Madonna and Kate Moss like to relax by picking up their knitting needles! Proven to be therapeutic for sufferers of stress and bereavement, knitting is also becoming a social activity – there are now around 462 knitting groups in the UK. Contact the UK Hand Knitting Association for more information www.ukhandknitting.com

L – Local history

Many people enjoy tracing their family tree, but looking into the history of your local area can be just as fascinating. Whether you've lived there all your life and fancy a trip down memory lane, or you've moved to a new area and want to see what it was like in times gone by, you'll find something for you. There are more than 1,000 local history societies in the UK, so it can be a good way to meet people locally too.

M –Mosaics

If you're into interior design, mosaics are a great way to update your home, as it looks gorgeous on anything from photo frames and decorative mirrors to vases and even house number signs. You may happen to have broken bits of ceramic hanging around the house, but if you don't, mosaic kits are available from good craft shops. If this is something you fancy introducing to your grandchildren, you'll also find 'sticky' mosaics for a safer alternative.

N – Nintendo Wii

It's only been around since 2006, but the Wii games console has proven a big hit with all ages. Research has shown that playing the active Wii Sports or Wii Fit games is great for older people, as much of the emphasis is on improving balance. As it combines mental and physical training, it's a perfect daily workout for both body and brain – in the comfort of your own home! Think fitness videos for the modern age.

P – Photography

Digital photography is now so popular that it is ranked in the top three university courses chosen by the over 60s. It's a hobby that you can practise no matter where you are, whether it's perfecting family snaps or making the most of your sightseeing holidays. Advance your skills even further by learning how to edit your images on your computer to make them truly show-stopping. Digital Photo magazine provides tips for all levels, available from all good newsagents.

O – Origami

Whether it was playing around with our schoolbooks, or transforming a serviette to entertain the children in a restaurant, we've all made a paper plane at some point in our lives. But the intricate Japanese art of paper folding has so much more to offer. Make a bunch of flowers to give to a loved one, a beautiful animal-themed table decoration, or hanging ornaments for next year's Christmas tree.

Q – Quilting

If your crafting skills are fairly advanced, or you fancy a challenge, then making a quilt could be right up your street. It's a more complex project, as it requires different types of sewing at various points along the way, and is time-consuming due to the sheer size of the object being made, but the finished product is well worth the effort. Why not make a personalised patchwork quilt as a family heirloom to cherish? ➥

R – Racketball

Racketball is the UK's fastest growing sport, and it's one that the more active among you may like to try out. The game is similar to squash, but played with a much larger ball and shorter racket. Because the ball moves slower, it gives the player more time to react to the shot, and the shorter racket allows for better hand/eye co-ordination, so it's a great option for older players. Many local sports centres offer over 50s racketball sessions, or visit www.uk-racketball.com for more information.

S –Sugarcraft

If you enjoy baking, learning the art of sugarcraft will enable you to decorate your creations, too. It involves using sugarpaste or fondant icing to make three dimensional decorations and centrepieces for your cakes, ranging from intricate flowers to models of animals or popular fictional characters. There is a range of equipment for this, from colour dusts to sculpting tools, meaning it isn't a cheap hobby, but most of these pieces can be used again and again.

T – Ten-pin bowling

It took us by storm in the Sixties, and there's no reason why ten-pin bowling shouldn't still be a thrill now. Many local bowling alleys offer senior discounts during quieter weekday periods, and it's a great way to get a group of friends together for a catch-up. If you want to get a bit more competitive, the British Ten Pin Bowling Association runs a Senior League. Go to www.btba.org.uk to find out more.

U – Upcycling

A fairly new phenomenon, upcycling involves taking an otherwise useless product, and converting it into something new that has more use and value. For example, jewellery can be made with anything from discarded drinks cans to old Scrabble tiles. Or, why not try turning glass bottles and jars into candle holders or vases? Great for the environment, it will also give your home that individual feel, and get your creative juices flowing.

V – Volunteering

Volunteering is a great way of devoting more time to any hobby or interest you may have. If you love animals, you could puppy walk for Guide Dogs for the Blind. A fashionista? Look into helping out at one of Oxfam's great vintage stores. Want to offer more practical help? Become a first aid worker with the St. John Ambulance. Volunteering England can give you many more ideas and resources – visit www.volunteering.org.uk or call 020 7713 6161.

W – Willow weaving

An ancient craft, willow woven baskets are perfect for the vintage, homely feel that is so popular in today's interior design. Some basket makers even grow their own willow, making this a truly 'back-to-basics' art. If you want to get involved, there are many local groups and evening courses to get you started. Contact the Basketmakers' Association for more – www.basketassoc.org

X − X-stitching

Okay, it's a slight cop-out, but this is as close to X as we can get! Cross-stitching is one of the most relaxing hobbies around, and with home crafts enjoying a resurgence since the recession, it's increasingly popular. It is relatively easy to create your own designs but if you're just getting started you may want to buy a cross-stitch kit, which provides a pattern for a particular picture or design, together with all the needles and cottons you need.

Y − Yoga

Yoga is great exercise for older people, as it helps to improve posture, balance and flexibility, as well as muscle tone. Making the joints more supple can also help prevent conditions we often face in later life, such as osteoporosis and arthritis. Most local fitness centres will offer a yoga class, and teachers will always encourage you to work at your own pace. Definitely worth a go to improve both body and mind!

Z − Zumba

It's the dance fitness craze that has swept the nation, and with good reason! Zumba takes Latin-inspired dance moves and puts them together in an aerobic style routine that makes keeping fit fun. On average, you can burn around 500 calories per hour doing a Zumba class. If you're worried it may be too energetic, try Zumba Gold – all the elements are the same, but the moves are modified slightly to make the pace more manageable.

Smarten up for

A tidy home is a happy home and now is the perfect time to get organised

Pretty practical

A handy noticeboard will help clear clutter from your kitchen worktops

You will need:

Pretty patterned fabric
A box canvas of your chosen size
Bias binding
Wadding
Scissors
Stapler and staples

1 Cut the wadding big enough to fit around your canvas, including the edges. For extra padding and depth, double the thickness of the wadding.

2 Staple the wadding to the back of the canvas on to the wooden rim, making sure you have pulled the wadding tight around the canvas to create a smooth surface. Take care on the corners to tuck the edges in neatly before stapling.

3 Repeat the first two steps and attach your chosen fabric in the same way so it covers the wadding completely. Trim any uneven edges for a neat finish.

4 Measure and cut the bias binding into strips that are large enough to create a diamond lattice over the top of your fabric. Check the lines of bias binding are parallel before stapling to the back of the canvas.

TOP TIP
Add detail to your noticeboard by decorating with pretty buttons.

spring

Don't forget!

Never lose your shopping list again with this stylish chalkboard

You will need:

Wooden photo frame
in a size of your choice
Wooden heart blanks
(or similar decorative items)
Chalk
Chalkboard paint, aerosol
Jute string
Sticky–backed black letters
Hot melt glue gun

1 Remove the backboard from the photo frame and spray the surface with several light coats of chalkboard paint allowing it to dry in between coats.
2 Spray a wooden heart shape in the same way ensuring the edges are also coated, then leave to dry.
3 Reassemble the frame (without the glass).
4 Cut a length of jute string of at least the height of your frame. Tie a stick of chalk to the end of the string and use the glue gun to glue the other end to the reverse of the heart
5 Apply a blob of hot glue to the reverse of the heart and position it on the frame corner.
6 Create a message of your choice using the sticky-backed black letters.

Handy shopper

You will need:

Plain calico bag
Fabric oddments
Black embroidery thread
Red satin ribbon
Red velvet ribbon
Red bead
Spray adhesive

1 First press your tote bag – iron on reverse.
2 Using the picture as a guide cut out the outline of the cat and two hearts from your chosen fabrics. Make sure they are big enough to appear prominently on the bag.
3 Spray adhesive lightly on the reverse and position the shapes on the bag.
4 Take a running stitch around the edge of each shape to hold it in position.
5 Create the cat's collar using red velvet ribbon and a bead, sewn in place. Finish by decorating the hearts with bows made from red satin ribbon.
6 Make the LOVE bag in the same way or use a stencil and dye the fabric for a neater finish.

TOP TIP
Once ironed, start by stuffing the bags with stiff cardboard so they hold shape while you're working on them.

Projects and photography courtesy of Hobbycraft (01202 596100, www.hobbycraft.co.uk).

A Year With **Yours** 2014   31

Pretty summer

Throw the perfect tea party with these finishing touches

Dotty Table Runner

This table runner is really simple but looks lovely

You will need

Fabric
Beads
Felt balls
Scissors
Sewing machine (or you can hand sew)
Needle
Thread

1 Measure and cut a length of fabric 30cm (12in) wide and 40cm (16in) longer than your table (to allow a drop of 20cm (8in) at each end). Double hem all sides of the fabric runner. You can do this by hand or a sewing machine will give a neater finish.
2 Next, sew a doubled-up length of cotton thread onto one corner of an end of the fabric runner and begin to thread a line of 5 small beads, finishing with a felt ball.
3 Then push the needle and thread back up through the felt ball and line of smaller beads and make a few neat stitches on the corner of the fabric again to secure the bead tassel in place.
4 Repeat with the other three corners of the fabric and then place along the centre of the table with tassels hanging down at each end.

Dotty Table Runner project and photography courtesy of Hobbycraft (01202 596100, www.hobbycraft.co.uk)

Vintage Teacup Card

This beautiful card makes a great party invitation or thank you card

You will need:

Stiff white card
Patterned paper
Decorative edge punch
White paper
Glue stick
Gold pen
Craft knife and cutting mat

1 Draw a teacup shape and cut out from thick white card with a craft knife. Fold the card in half down the centre.
2 Cut out a piece of floral patterned paper following the bowl section of the teacup and glue onto your white folded card.
3 Cut out a piece of striped paper following the lower portion of the teacup and glue in place.
4 Use the edge punch to cut a scalloped strip 2cm (¾in) deep along the edge of the white paper. Ensure that your strip is long enough to cover the width of the cup.
5 Glue the white paper to the top of the card and trim the edges to fit. Draw decorative details on the top rim, base and handle with a gold pen.
6. Leave the back white or repeat steps 2–5 to decorate the back of the card in the same way.

TOP TIP
If you're feeling extra creative why not try a teapot shaped card, too!

party projects

Easy Paper Bunting

Decorate your home with this no-sew alternative to fabric bunting

You will need:

Patterned paper
Decorative ribbons
Decorative edge punch
Glue stick
Hole punch
Scissors

1 Cut two triangles for each bunting flag from co-ordinating patterned papers. The more triangles you choose to make, the longer your bunting will be.

2 Cut strips of a contrasting paper 2.5cm (1inch) wide. You'll need four strips for each of your triangles. Punch the strips with a scallop border punch to create a decorative edge. Glue two strips wrong sides together to make them double-sided – the pattern only should be showing now.

3 Glue one strip to each side of a triangle on the un-patterned side of the paper. The scalloped edge should overhang the edge of the triangle by about 1cm. Glue the matching triangle of patterned paper over the glued edges of the strips to cover them up and create a double-sided bunting flag. Repeat for the remaining paper triangles and strips.

4 Use a hole punch to cut out one hole on either side of the top edge of your bunting flags.

5 Cut lengths of ribbon 60cm (24in) long. Thread a length of ribbon through the right-hand hole of one bunting flag, from the back to the front. Put the other end through the left-hand hole of the next bunting flag and tie the two ends together in a bow.

6 Trim the ends of the ribbon

so that they are even, creating an inverted v-shape. Continue in this way to add more flags until your bunting is the desired length.

Vintage Teacup Card and Pretty Paper Bunting projects by Prudence Rogers, taken from 101 Ways To Stitch Craft Create (published by David & Charles) and inspired by www.stitchcraftcreate.co.uk

Easy makes for

Enjoy evenings curled up on the sofa with these homely crafts

Autumnal tweed

This super-cute doorstop is really simple to make

You will need:

4 x 50x20cm (20x8in) pieces of medium-weight
iron-on interfacing
4 different pieces of tweed fabric each 50x20cm (20x8in)
Polyester toy filling
Dried peas
10-15 buttons to decorate
Take in 1cm seam allowances throughout, unless otherwise stated.

1 Following the manufacturer's instructions, apply interfacing to the wrong side of all the tweed pieces. Cut a rectangle paper template 18x6cm and cut six rectangles from each fabric.

2 With right sides together, pin and stitch the rectangles of four different fabrics together along one long side to make a square. Press the seams open and repeat with the leftover strips to make six squares.

3 To make the tab, cut two 14x4.5cm rectangles of fabric. With right sides together, pin and stitch along the long edges leaving the short ends open. Turn right side out and press. Fold the tab in half to form a loop. Align the raw edges, pin and tack the loop to the centre of the right side of one of the two remaining square widths.

4 With right sides together (alternating the directions of the strips) pin and stitch four squares together to make a long strip. Press seams open. With right sides together, pin and stitch the short ends of the long strip together to form an open-ended cube. Press the seam open.

5 With right sides together, pin one of the remaining squares onto one end of the cube, aligning the corners of the square with the seams of the cube. Stitch in place, starting and finishing 1cm from the edges. Make a small snip at each corner as you sew. Turn right side out and press.

6 Turn wrong side out again and pin and stitch the last square in place as in step 5, leaving a gap of 8cm along the bottom edge. Turn the cube right side out and press. Fill with two thirds toy filling and the remaining space with dried peas. Stitch the gap closed.

7 Decorate by stitching two or three buttons onto the top and each side of the cube.

Doorstop project and images from Super-cute Doorstops by Emma Hardy. Photography by Debbie Patterson. Published by CICO books, rrp £12.99.

a cosy home

As easy as ABC

Brighten up a dull room
with this pretty cushion

You will need:

0.5m white fabric
0.5m red floral fabric
Iron on adhesive
15in cushion pad
Machine thread – white

1 Cut two 40cm square panels from
   the white fabric and set one aside.
2 Draw your chosen initial onto a large piece of
   paper or card and cut out. Turn the letter over
   and draw around this shape on the paper side of
   the iron on adhesive.
3 Cut out and iron onto the reverse of the floral
   fabric. Bond the initial to the centre of one of the
   cushion panels with an iron.
4 Place the two panels back to back (right sides
   together), pin and machine stitch a seam around
   three sides 1cm from the edge. Insert pad and slip
   stitch seam closed.

TOP TIP

Make an envelope-type back to the panel which
overlaps and enables pad to be removed from
cover for washing.

Hanging hearts

These scented hearts make great gifts

You will need

Quarter metres of fabric
Buttons
Thread
60cm narrow ribbon
Lavender for filling

1 Freehand draw a heart shape. Make it slightly
   bigger than you'd like your heart to end up as
   you'll need to leave a 1cm seam allowance round
   the edges. Use this template to cut three pairs of
   identical hearts in co-ordinating fabrics.
2 Pin each pair right sides together and stitch
   round the heart shape leaving a small opening
   through which to insert the lavender.
3 Turn right side out and fill with the lavender,
   then close the opening by hand with a few
   stitches. Sew a button onto each and add a
   hanging loop made from 20cm ribbon.

Cushion and lavender heart projects and photography courtesy of
Hobbycraft (01202 596100, www.hobbycraft.co.uk).

Have a creative

Get in to the festive spirit with these seasonally inspired crafts

Hanging Pud

Who could resist this charming tree decoration?

You will need:

Brown, green and white felt
Red felt embellishments
White, brown and green sewing thread
Red stranded cotton
Polyester wadding

1 Cut one 23cm diameter circle and one 4cm diameter circle from brown felt. Cut three holly leaf shapes from green felt and one icing piece from white felt. The icing needs to be circular and roughly half the size of the larger brown felt circle. Remember to make it look like the icing is dripping – you can draw this freehand as it doesn't need to be perfect.

2 Hand sew the white icing piece to the centre of the large brown circle using white sewing thread. Make a hanging loop with red stranded cotton by sewing through the middle of the icing and back through again, then knotting the ends together on the inside.

3 Hand sew around the large brown circle with a running stitch, about 3mm from the edge, using brown sewing thread. Pull your stitches tightly to gather the felt as you go.

TOP TIP

This would make a great gift for friends and family to hang on their trees.

4 With the needle and thread on the outside, stuff the felt with polyester wadding and pull the gathers tightly to form a pudding shape. Stitch at the bottom to hold in place. Neatly sew the smaller circle of felt over the base to finish.

5 Embroider the centre of the holly leaves with running stitch using green sewing thread. Sew the holly leaves and red felt embellishments to the top using the red stranded cotton and green sewing thread.

Christmas Pudding Tree Decoration by Sue Trevor, taken from 101 Ways To Stitch Craft Create (published by David & Charles) and inspired by www.stitchcraftcreate.co.uk.

Christmas

Ribbon card

This card looks great and is so easy to make your grandkids can help too!

You will need:

A5 red card folded in half
White embossed paper
Brown corduroy card
A selection of red and white ribbons
Red stick-on felt
Double sided tape
Glue

1 Cut and stick a rectangular piece of white dotty embossed paper onto the front of your red folded card.
2 Draw a triangular tree shape on the back of a piece of brown corduroy card and cut out.
3 Decorate the tree with ribbon stripes, alternating colours and patterns and leaving a small gap between each. Stick on using double sided tape. Trim the ends of the tape and stick the tree to the card.
4 Cut out a red felt star, and stick to the top of the tree.

With love...

This inexpensive project would make a lovely gift for that special someone

You will need:

A plain white or cream frame
A heart shaped mount (available from craft stores)
Word stamps
Heart shaped adhesive gems and tiny black buttons to decorate if desired
Alphabet stickers
Glue

1 On a sheet of paper that fits behind the heart shaped mount lightly trace the heart outline.
2 Working within the heart shape, stamp on lettering and fill the spaces with gems, buttons and letter stickers. For this example they used a calligraphic style stamp available from craft stores.
3 You could make up your own sentiments by printing them out from your computer and simply cut it to fit your frame. It doesn't matter if the words don't fit in the heart gap perfectly.
4 Allow the glued buttons to dry before securing inside the frame.

TOP TIP

Use quotes from love poems, fill it with special dates, honeymoon or travel destinations.

Ribbon Tree Greetings Card and Heart Frame project and photography courtesy of Hobbycraft (01202 596100, www.hobbycraft.co.uk).

Facts and figures

Here are some handy conversion tables for cooks

Dry weight

IMPERIAL	METRIC
½ oz	15 g
1 oz	25 g
2 oz	50 g
3 oz	75 g
4 oz	110 g
5 oz	150 g
6 oz	175 g
7 oz	200 g
8 oz	225 g
9 oz	250 g
10 oz	275 g
11 oz	300 g
12 oz	350 g
13 oz	375 g
14 oz	400 g
15 oz	425 g
1 lb	450 g
1 lb 2 oz	500 g
1 ½ lb	680 g
1lb 10oz	750 g
2 lb	900 g

Liquid

IMPERIAL	METRIC
½ fl oz	15 ml
1 fl oz	30 ml
2 fl oz	60 ml
3 fl oz	90 ml
4 fl oz	125 ml
5 fl oz (¼ pint)	150 ml
6 fl oz	175 ml
8 fl oz	225 ml
10 fl oz (¼ pint)	300 ml
12 fl oz	350 ml
16 fl oz	450 ml
18 fl oz	500 ml
20 fl oz (1 pint)	600 ml
1 ½ pints	900 ml
1 ¾ pints	1 litre
2 pints	1.25 litres
2 ½ pints	1.5 litres
3 ½ pints	2 litres

Oven temperatures

°C	°C with fan	°F	Gas Mark
110	90	225	¼
120/130	100/110	250	½
140	120	275	1
150	130	300	2
160/170	140/150	325	3
180	160	350	4
190	170	375	5
200	180	400	6
220	200	425	7
230	210	450	8
240	220	475	9

Other equivalents

Dash	$1/16$ teaspoon
Pinch	$1/8$ teaspoon
1 tablespoon	3 teaspoons
$1/8$ cup	2 tablespoons
$1/4$ cup	4 tablespoons
$1/3$ cup	5 tablespoons plus 1 teaspoon
$1/2$ cup	8 tablespoons
$3/4$ cup	12 tablespoons
1 cup	16 tablespoons or 8 fl oz

Cake tin sizes

Round tin		Square tin	
6 inches	15 cm	5 inch	13 cm
8 inches	20 cm	7 inch	18 cm
9 inches	23 cm	8 inches	20 cm
11 inches	28 cm	10 inches	25.5 cm

Healthy eating

Guideline daily amounts for adults

Women should aim to eat no more than 2,000 kcal each day (men 2,500 kcal)
– spaced across the day this would be:
400 kcal at breakfast (including drinks)
600 kcal at lunch (including drinks)
600kcal for your evening meal (including drinks)
no more than 400 kcal for healthy snacks

The guidelines (below) will help you identify if a product is high in fat, saturated fat, salt or sugar or not.

Total fat
High = more than 20g of fat per 100g
Low = 3g of fat or less per 100g
Saturated fat
High = more than 5g of saturated fat per 100g
Low = 1.5g of saturated fat or less per 100g
Sugars
High = more than 15g of total sugars per 100g
Low = 5g of total sugars or less per 100g
Salt
High = more than 1.5g of salt per 100g (or 0.6g sodium)
Low = 0.3g of salt or less per 100g (or 0.1g sodium)

How to get your five a day

We all know that for optimum health we should eat five portions of fruit and veg a day – but what is a portion?

A portion of fruit (80g) is roughly equivalent to:
A slice of melon
Half a grapefruit.
1 medium size fruit for example an apple.
2 small size fruits such as plums or satsumas.

A portion of dried fruit (30g) is roughly equivalent to:
a heaped tablespoon of dried fruit

A portion of vegetables (80g) is roughly equivalent to:
3 heaped tablespoons of peas, beans or pulses.
2 broccoli spears.
a dessert bowl of salad.

For more advice on healthy eating visit either www.nhs.uk/livewell or www.nhs.uk/Change4Life

Notable dates 2014

BANK HOLIDAY	Wednesday January 1
Epiphany	Monday January 6
Burns' Night	Saturday January 25
Chinese New Year (Horse)	Friday January 31
Valentine's Day	Friday February 14
St David's Day	Saturday March 1
Shrove Tuesday (Pancake Day)	Tuesday March 4
Ash Wednesday	Wednesday March 5
Commonwealth Day	Monday March 10
St Patrick's Day	Monday March 17
Bank Holiday (N. Ireland/Eire)	Monday March 17
Mothering Sunday	Sunday March 30
British Summertime begins (clocks go forward)	Sunday March 30
Palm Sunday	Sunday April 13
GOOD FRIDAY	Friday April 18
Easter Day	Sunday April 20
BANK HOLIDAY (Easter Monday)	Monday April 21
St George's Day	Wednesday April 23
BANK HOLIDAY	Monday May 5
BANK HOLIDAY	Monday May 26
Ascension Day	Thursday May 29
Fathers' Day	Sunday June 15
Summer Solstice (Longest day)	Saturday June 21
Wimbledon Tennis Tournament begins	Monday June 23
Armed Forces Day	Saturday June 28
First Day of Ramadan (Islam)	Sunday June 29
American Independence Day	Friday July 4
Battle of the Boyne (Holiday N. Ireland)	Monday July 14
St Swithun's Day	Tuesday July 15
Bank Holiday (Eire and Scotland)	Monday August 4
BANK HOLIDAY	Monday August 25
Jewish New Year	Thursday September 25
Trafalgar Day	Tuesday October 21
Islamic New Year	Saturday October 25
British Summertime ends (clocks go back)	Sunday October 26
Bank Holiday (Eire)	Monday October 27
Diwali (Hindu Festival)	Thursday October 23
Hallowe'en	Friday October 31
Remembrance Sunday	Sunday November 9
St Andrew's Day	Sunday November 30
First Sunday in Advent	Sunday November 30
Winter Solstice (Shortest day)	Sunday December 21
CHRISTMAS DAY	Thursday December 25
BOXING DAY	Friday December 26
New Year's Eve/Hogmanay	Wednesday December 31

Sunrise & sunset times

	SUNRISE	SUNSET
Jan 1	8:06 am	4:02 pm
Feb 1	7:39 am	4:50 pm
Mar 1	6:45 am	5:41 pm
April 1	6:36 am	7:34 pm
May 1	5:32 am	8:24 pm
June 1	4:49 am	9:08 pm
July 1	4:48 am	9:21 pm
Aug 1	5:24 am	8:48 pm
Sept 1	6:13 am	7:47 pm
Oct 1	7:01 am	6:38 pm
Nov 1	6:54 am	4:33 pm
Dec 1	7:44 am	3:55 pm

Birthstones & flowers

Month	Stone	Flower
January	Garnet	Carnation
February	Amethyst	Violet
March	Aquamarine	Jonquil or Daffodil
April	Diamond	Sweet Pea
May	Emerald	Lily of the Valley
June	Pearl	Rose
July	Ruby	Larkspur
August	Peridot	Gladioli
September	Sapphire	Aster
October	Opal	Calendula
November	Topaz	Chrysanthemum
December	Turquoise	Narcissus

Anniversaries

1	PAPER
2	COTTON
3	LEATHER
4	BOOKS
5	WOOD
6	IRON
7	WOOL
8	BRONZE
9	COPPER
10	TIN
11	STEEL
12	SILK
13	LACE
14	IVORY
15	CRYSTAL
20	CHINA
25	SILVER
30	PEARL
35	CORAL
40	RUBY
45	SAPPHIRE
50	GOLDEN
55	EMERALD
60	DIAMOND
65	BLUE SAPPHIRE
70	PLATINUM

Signs of the zodiac

AQUARIUS	PISCES	ARIES	TAURUS	GEMINI	CANCER
Jan 21–Feb 18	Feb 19–Mar 20	Mar 21–Apr 20	Apr 21–May 21	May 22–June 21	June 22–July 22

LEO	VIRGO	LIBRA	SCORPIO	SAGITTARIUS	CAPRICORN
July 23–Aug 23	Aug 24–Sept 22	Sept 23–Oct 23	Oct 24–Nov 22	Nov 23–Dec 21	Dec 22–Jan 20

2014 year-to-view calendar

JANUARY

M		6	13	20	27
Tu		7	14	21	28
W	1	8	15	22	29
Th	2	9	16	23	30
F	3	10	17	24	31
Sa	4	11	18	25	
Su	5	12	19	26	

FEBRUARY

M		3	10	17	24
Tu		4	11	18	25
W		5	12	19	26
Th		6	13	20	27
F		7	14	21	28
Sa	1	8	15	22	
Su	2	9	16	23	

MARCH

M		3	10	17	24	31
Tu		4	11	18	25
W		5	12	19	26
Th		6	13	20	27
F		7	14	21	28
Sa	1	8	15	22	29
Su	2	9	16	23	30

APRIL

M		7	14	21	28
Tu	1	8	15	22	29
W	2	9	16	23	30
Th	3	10	17	24	
F	4	11	18	25	
Sa	5	12	19	26	
Su	6	13	20	27	

MAY

M		5	12	19	26
Tu		6	13	20	27
W		7	14	21	28
Th	1	8	15	22	29
F	2	9	16	23	30
Sa	3	10	17	24	31
Su	4	11	18	25	

JUNE

M		2	9	16	23	30
Tu		3	10	17	24
W		4	11	18	25
Th		5	12	19	26
F		6	13	20	27
Sa		7	14	21	28
Su	1	8	15	22	29

JULY

M		7	14	21	28
Tu	1	8	15	22	29
W	2	9	16	23	30
Th	3	10	17	24	31
F	4	11	18	25	
Sa	5	12	19	26	
Su	6	13	20	27	

AUGUST

M		4	11	18	25
Tu		5	12	19	26
W		6	13	20	27
Th		7	14	21	28
F	1	8	15	22	29
Sa	2	9	16	23	30
Su	3	10	17	24	31

SEPTEMBER

M	1	8	15	22	29
Tu	2	9	16	23	30
W	3	10	17	24	
Th	4	11	18	25	
F	5	12	19	26	
Sa	6	13	20	27	
Su	7	14	21	28	

OCTOBER

M		6	13	20	27
Tu		7	14	21	28
W	1	8	15	22	29
Th	2	9	16	23	30
F	3	10	16	24	31
Sa	4	11	18	25	
Su	5	12	19	26	

NOVEMBER

M		3	10	17	24
Tu		4	11	18	25
W		5	12	19	26
Th		6	13	20	27
F		7	14	21	28
Sa	1	8	15	22	29
Su	2	9	16	23	30

DECEMBER

M	1	8	15	22	29
Tu	2	9	16	23	30
W	3	10	17	24	31
Th	4	11	18	25	
F	5	12	19	26	
Sa	6	13	20	27	
Su	7	14	21	28	

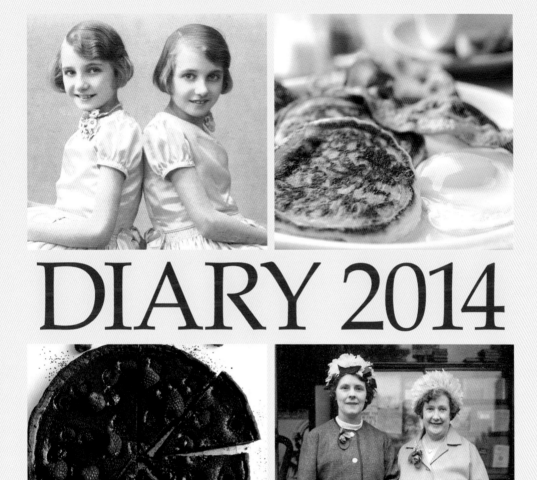

DIARY 2014

30 Monday

31 Tuesday

1 Wednesday

2 Thursday

3 Friday

4 Saturday

5 Sunday

Every picture tells a story

Liz look-alikes

When I was 15 I so wanted to be like Elizabeth Taylor. I was told that I looked like her but the milkman who delivered the milk to our school used to call me Margaret Lockwood because he thought I looked like her. I wanted to be an actress, but my parents couldn't afford to send me to drama school – I had to go out to work to earn my keep.

Valerie Temple, Great Dunmow, Essex

I loved films with Elizabeth Taylor in them. She was always dressed beautifully with glamorous jewellery. When I went ballroom dancing I used to wear lovely dresses made with diamanté and sequins. Although I am older now, I still dress up in evening clothes with make-up and nice jewellery. People say I have same look as Elizabeth. Pity I haven't got her money, diamonds and rubies – but then again, I have held onto the same husband for 40 years and that means more to me!

Barbara Nuttall, Bolton, Lancs

Home hints

If you haven't already done so, dig planting areas in your garden before the weather gets colder and the frosts start. If you have rhubarb cover it with an old bucket to encourage early growth. At the end of this month start chitting your potatoes – they'll be ready to plant in roughly six weeks.

Wise words

"Don't put it down, put it away"
I read this many years ago and it really struck a cord. It is tricky to stick to but it's such a simple way of keeping things tidy. **Mrs E N Bates, Leicester**

Headgear of yesteryear

This is a 1930s photo of my grandma and granddad looking very suave. Mary and Alfred Mackwood were a devoted, caring and beautiful couple. Here they are dressed in a traditional yet fashionable style – I think the dress sense was more refined in those days compared with today's fashion trends. I love my granddad's trilby, and think it really finished off a very smart outdoor outfit.
Anita Mackwood, Bradford, West Yorkshire

On this week...

December 31, 1964 – Campbell breaks own record
Daredevil Donald Campbell reached an average speed of 276.33mph (444.71km/h), on Lake Dumbleyung, Western Australia, in his famed speedboat, Bluebird. This amazing feat shattered his own previous world record of 260.35mph (418.99km/h) set at Lake Coniston, Cumbria, in 1959. "I never thought we had the chance of a snowball on the desert of cracking it today," the record breaker said afterwards.

Recipe of the week

Macadamia and Turkey Risotto

Serves: 4
Preparation time: 15 minutes
Cooking time: 30 minutes
1 onion, peeled and sliced
1 clove garlic, peeled and finely chopped
2 tbsp macadamia oil
1 red pepper, deseeded and sliced
180g (6 1/4oz) risotto rice
600ml (21fl.oz) warm vegetable stock
200g (7oz) cooked turkey, shredded
200g (7oz) green vegetables – broccoli, green beans, sugar snap peas, blanched
100g (3 1/2oz) macadamia nuts, chopped (toasted if preferred)
Salt and pepper
Fresh parsley, to garnish

1 Fry the onion and garlic in 1 tbsp oil, in a large pan, for a couple of minutes. Add the pepper and cook until the onion has softened.
2 Stir in rice, coating well with oil, then pour in about 200ml (7fl.oz) stock. Cook over a medium heat, stirring occasionally, until the stock is almost absorbed. Then, keep adding stock while stirring until the rice is just tender. This will take around 20 minutes.
3 Stir in chicken and warm through, then add vegetables and nuts. Season to taste. Serve hot, with parsley and a drizzle of macadamia oil.
© The Macadamia Advice Centre, www.macadamias.org.uk

6	Monday

7	Tuesday

8	Wednesday

9	Thursday

10	Friday

11	Saturday

12	Sunday

Every picture tells a story

Keeping it 'hush-hush'

I was still at school when the Second World War began. At the age of 16 we had to register for National Service and at 17 I volunteered to join the Women's Royal Naval Service (WRNS).

In 1944, after training, I was sent to Station X, now known to be the secret decoding station at Bletchley Park. It was many miles from the sight of the sea and ships but the work was interesting.

It was too secret for us to talk about what we did and for 30 years after the war we still had to remain silent.

When the European conflict was over I was transferred from German signals to Japanese signals and volunteered to be sent overseas. I was posted to Ceylon (now Sri Lanka), an island of warmth and colour in great contrast to the drabness of wartime Britain.

There was sun and sea, wonderful fresh fruit and no rationing. It was there that I met my future husband. At the end of the war we returned to the UK, married and set up home.

Gwendoline Page,
Swaffham, Norfolk

Home hints

Munch on healthy immune-boosting foods to keep colds and other nasty bugs at bay. Garlic and onions are both great choices, as they contain antibacterial and antiviral properties. For best results eat them raw, or lightly cook and add them to just about any dish.

Wise words

"You just have to let it go… then keep letting it go"
When complaining to a stranger at a party about my husband's peculiar habits, her advice came to me out of the blue and at just the right time.

Nina Oakman, by email

Headgear of yesteryear

Here is a photo of me and my youngest daughter, Laura, when she was around five years old, in 1992. We were camping with the Girls' Brigade in Filey, North Yorkshire. On Sundays, we always marched to the local Methodist church for Sunday Service, and I played the bass drum in the band. Laura loved the huge banging it made! I have now been an Officer in the Girls' Brigade for 40 years.

Anne Bradder, via email

On this week...

January 6, 1977 – Sex Pistols given the sack
Notorious punk group the Sex Pistols were fired by their record label for their unacceptable behaviour in public. The final straw had been reports of them swearing at staff at Heathrow Airport and spitting at each other as they waited to board a flight. In June they released their single God Save the Queen on Richard Branson's Virgin record label. The record got to number two despite being banned by BBC Radio 1 and several high-street chains.

Recipe of the week

Vegetarian Tikka

Serves: 4
Preparation time:
15 minutes, plus 30 minutes marinating
Cooking time: 30 minutes

For the marinade
2 tbsp tikka paste
1 tbsp each of ground coriander, ground cumin, and turmeric
1 tsp chilli powder
150ml (5 $\frac{1}{4}$fl.oz) natural yoghurt
1 tbsp tomato purée
2 cloves garlic, crushed

300g (10 $\frac{1}{2}$oz) Quorn Chicken style pieces
1tbsp vegetable oil
1 onion, chopped
400ml (14fl.oz) vegetable stock
1 sweet potato, peeled and cut into small cubes
100g (3 $\frac{1}{2}$oz) baby spinach leaves
Coriander leaves, to garnish
Brown rice and mango chutney, to serve

1. Combine marinade ingredients and stir in the Quorn (or meat, for a non-vegetarian dish, if you prefer). Leave to marinate for at least 30 minutes or overnight.
2. Heat oil and sauté onion for 2-3 minutes until soft. Add the Quorn, along with the marinade and cook for 5 minutes, stirring, to warm the spices.
3. Gradually add the stock, then the sweet potato. Bring to the boil then simmer, covered, for 15 minutes or until the sweet potato is tender.
4. Add the spinach and stir until wilted, then season to taste and garnish with fresh coriander. Serve with brown rice and mango chutney.

© Quorn, www.quorn.co.uk

13 Monday

14 Tuesday

15 Wednesday

16 Thursday

17 Friday

18 Saturday

19 Sunday

Every picture tells a story

PIC: REX FEATURES

Still smitten at 70

I had just turned 12 and was not very interested in the cinema unless it was to see George Formby or Old Mother Riley. However, my mother insisted on taking me to see a film called Caravan. We queued for two hours in the rain. When the gipsy girl, played by Jean Kent, came on, I was mesmerised. I joined her fan club and went to see every film she had made.

When she returned to the stage, I wrote to her at every theatre she appeared in and continued to write to her from Malaya where I did my National Service. On my return to England, I thought it was about time I met my idol so I went to see her in Manchester, but at the stage door I lost my nerve and started to walk away. I turned back, was directed to the star's dressing room, and came face to face with the beautiful smile that had lit up the screen all those years ago. We conversed and she made me feel very special. I'm in my 70s now but when I think of the first time I saw Jean Kent, it's still magic.

R Taylor, Merseyside

Home hints

Control chocolate cravings. Cutting down doesn't have to mean no chocolate whatsoever – just choose your choc fix wisely. Try dark chocolate, which has a higher cocoa content so more taste and less calories. Or, how about a low-fat chocolate mousse or low-calorie hot chocolate? Both great ways to enjoy the taste without the guilt.

Wise words

"Always be honest with your doctor"
My father always told me; 'a priest will forgive you but a doctor could harm you with the wrong medicine if you're not truthful'. Good advice I think.

Marie McKay, Luton

Headgear of yesteryear

This photo of my mother (on the left in the picture) was taken when she was a nurse in London during the Blitz. She is wearing one of her prized collection of hats. I once asked her what had happened to them and she told me that one afternoon, on a sudden impulse and later deeply regretted, she had given them all away. After that, she didn't have the heart to buy any more hats until the Fifties when another photo shows her wearing a smart little hat at a cocktail party. **Mary Reeve, Cardigan**

On this week...

January 14, 1969 – Sir Matt Busby announces his retirement
Football legend Sir Matt Busby announced he would retire as manager of Manchester United at the end of the season. Sir Matt told a press conference at the club's ground, Old Trafford: "It's time to make way for a younger man... a track-suited manager." However, his successors struggled to live up to the Busby name until Tommy Docherty took the helm in 1972.

Recipe of the week

Cranberry and Ginger Cookies

Makes: approx. 42 cookies
Preparation time: 30 minutes
Cooking time: 9–12 minutes

175g (6 $^1/_4$oz) sugar
75g (3oz) brown sugar
100g (3 $^1/_2$oz) butter or margarine, softened
75ml (3fl.oz) milk
1 large egg
275g (9 $^3/_4$oz) plain flour
$^1/_2$ tsp baking powder
$^1/_2$ tsp ground ginger
$^1/_4$ tsp bicarbonate of soda
150g (5 $^1/_4$oz) dried cranberries
75g (3oz) chopped pecans
50g (2oz) finely chopped crystallised ginger
For the glaze
350g (12 $^1/_4$oz) icing sugar
1 to 2 tbsp milk

1 Preheat oven to 190˚C/375˚F/Gas Mark 5. Lightly grease baking sheets.
2 Combine sugar, brown sugar and butter in a large mixing bowl and beat until well mixed. Add milk and egg and beat until smooth.
3 Add flour, baking powder, ground ginger and bicarbonate of soda and again, beat until well mixed. Gently stir in the dried cranberries, pecans and crystallised ginger.
4 Drop dough in rounded teaspoonfuls, 5cm (2in) apart, onto the sheets. Bake for 9 to 12 minutes, until the edges of the cookies are a light golden–brown. Immediately remove and cool on a wire rack.
5 In a small bowl, combine icing sugar and enough milk for desired glaze consistency. Drizzle glaze over cooled cookies.
© Ocean Spray, www.oceanspray.co.uk

20 Monday

21 Tuesday

22 Wednesday

23 Thursday

24 Friday

25 Saturday

26 Sunday

Every picture tells a story

Granny's bedtime tales

My Granny Minty was always a great inspiration to me and sadly died when I was only 17. I wasn't really old enough to appreciate the many wise words and kindnesses that she passed on to me. I remember snuggling up to her in bed when I was little and she told me amazing stories about fairies in the woods and elves having tea parties. I remember that they ate so many delicious cakes that they were often sick afterwards (this may have had something to do with trying to curb my voracious appetite!).

I have always loved writing and after selling short stories and articles, I have finally published a novel. I believe the imagination I needed to do this came from her. I couldn't believe how words, phrases and ideas sometimes flew into my head and on to the page and I'm sure I know where they came from. Thank you, Grandma Minty, you are still coming through loud and clear!

Lynne Whelon, Carnforth, Lancs

On this week...

January 24, 1961 – Marilyn Monroe divorces – again
Hollywood legend Marilyn Monroe divorced her third husband, the American playwright, Arthur Miller, after less than five years of marriage. The couple had been working together on her last film, The Misfits, and there were rumours of arguments on set. Marilyn had previously been married to baseball star Joe DiMaggio but their tempestuous marriage lasted just nine months.

Home hints

Beat the January doldrums with a mood-boosting trip down memory lane. While chocolate and listening to your favourite music are both thought to boost your mood, it's flicking through your old photo albums that experts have found gives us the most uplifting emotions.

Wise words

"The most precious gift you can give a child is your time"
My GP said this to me when my children were small and I always tried to bear it in mind. My children are grown up now with children of their own and we all have a wonderful relationship.
Beryl Kelsey, Upminster

Headgear of yesteryear

This was when my granddaughter, Jessi, was almost three. Although the headgear is not conventional, Jessi was convinced it was. Her mum had been cleaning her baby sister Erin's cot, and asked Jessi to hold the mobile for a moment. It promptly found a new home, and by good luck I was there with my ever-ready camera! Jessi is now 22 years old and this is not her favourite photo, but I wouldn't part with it for anything.
June Williams, St. Helen's, Merseyside

Recipe of the week

Creamy Mushroom Tagliatelle
Serves: 4
Preparation time: 5 minutes
Cooking time: 15–20 minutes

350g (12 ¼oz) tagliatelle
Knob of butter
1 tbsp olive oil
3 cloves garlic, chopped
500g (1lb 1 ½oz) chestnut mushrooms, quartered
Salt and pepper
4 large eggs
300ml (10 ½fl.oz) cream
75g (3oz) Parmesan, grated
3 tbsp fresh chives, chopped

1 Cook the tagliatelle in a large pan of boiling salted water for about 10 minutes or according to packet instructions, until 'al dente'.
2 Meanwhile, heat the butter and oil together in a large frying pan, then sizzle the garlic for 30 seconds before adding the mushrooms. Cook over high heat for 6–8 minutes, stirring occasionally until the mushrooms are nicely browned. Remove from heat and season to taste.
3 Lightly beat together the eggs and cream, stir in half of the Parmesan and season to taste.
4 Drain the pasta in a colander and return to the pan. Stir in the egg mixture, garlic mushrooms and chives, and toss together. The heat from the pasta will lightly thicken the sauce.
5 Top with the remaining Parmesan to serve.
© Silvana Franco, www.moretomushrooms.co.uk

27 Monday

28 Tuesday

29 Wednesday

30 Thursday

31 Friday

1 Saturday

2 Sunday

Every picture tells a story

A winter wonderland?

This photo was taken in 1940 in the village of Denby in Yorkshire. My sister, Joan, and I are pictured with other children on our way home from school. Joan is on the right in the back row and I am on the left in the middle row. We lived in the village of Ingbirchworth where my father was in charge of the filtration plant on the nearby reservoir. Our home was a mile away from the school and it was a long cold walk.

If the heating was off we were told to bring extra clothes to keep warm. The snow on the road was not moved by a lorry with a plough attached, but by two horses pulling a wooden plough. The plough did not go in a straight line as when the snow built up on one side it went slightly sideways, leaving a zig zag on the side of the road. This was then straightened by local prisoners of war. The cleared snow formed a wall on the side of the road which we children walked along if we set out before the plough had been through.

John Green, Exmouth, Devon

On this week...

February 1, 1984 – Farewell half penny
After 13 years in circulation, it was announced that the half penny coin was to be withdrawn. One of the main reasons for the coin's demise was that the cost of making it was higher than its face value. There were about 2.5 billion half pennies still in circulation when the announcement was made, many of them lurking down the back of our sofas or in charity boxes.

Home hints

Make pots for seedlings out of eggshell halves. Gently wash and dry them and use a pin to make a very small hole in the bottom for drainage. Keep them in the egg box so they are nice and stable, fill them with soil then plant your seed. When they're ready you can plant them straight into the ground.

Wise words

"I shall pass through this world but once. Any good that I can do, or kindness that I can show, let me do it now. Let me not defer or neglect it, for I shall not pass this way again"

I was given a framed copy of these words when I left teacher training college in India and still have them 50 years later.　　**Evelyn Webb, Cambridge**

Headgear of yesteryear

My father-in-law, John, never went anywhere without his flat cap – even if he was just walking to the bottom of the garden, the cap would go on! This is a lovely photo of him outside the house where we used to live around 40 years ago, when my daughter was little. My husband's family lived just over an hour away in Lincolnshire, and would often come to visit for the day.

Sheila Manterfield, via email

Recipe of the week

Sweet Chilli Chicken Thighs

Serves: 4
Preparation time: 10 minutes
Cooking time: 20 minutes

4 chicken thighs
1 onion, sliced
1 pack mixed peppers, all deseeded and cut into slices
1 piece fresh ginger, peeled and sliced thinly
2 tbsp vegetable oil
25ml (1fl.oz) water
300g (10 ¹/₂oz) jar sweet chilli sauce
To serve
Sticky white rice and Asian vegetables

1 Add the oil to a hot wok, then the onions to cook off first.
2 Put the chicken thighs in, skin side down, and cook for 5 minutes on each side until golden. Add the water at this stage to prevent the chicken burning.
3 Add the peppers and stir through until warmed, then pour over the sweet chilli sauce.
4 Cook for a further 10 minutes – the sauce will thicken and create a glaze over the thighs. Make sure the chicken thigh is fully cooked by skewering the thickest part – when the juices run clear, the chicken is cooked. Continue for another minute or so to warm through completely.
© Sweet Mandarin, www.sweetmandarin.net

3	Monday

4	Tuesday

5	Wednesday

6	Thursday

7	Friday

8	Saturday

9	Sunday

Every picture tells a story

Fun on the farm

This house, West Farm, is where I was born in 1931. We had no electricity, telephone or indoor bathroom. The only water we had came from the roofs of buildings down into a filter bed then into a tank under the lawn from where it was pumped up and transported in buckets. Most of the farm work was done by two shire horses, Blossom and Sharper.

We had many black cats, although they never came near enough to stroke. Their job was to keep down rats and mice. We made our own butter in a big churn in the dairy and also had lots of eggs. In the kitchen, the big fire range was always alight with kettles singing on the hob. My best friend lived half a mile away. We had much fun playing in the fields and woods, picking mushrooms and wild flowers. In the long winter evenings, the family played billiards in the front room which was lit by oil lamps so we had to be very careful not to knock them over with a ball.

Jean Virgo, Swindon, Wiltshire

On this week...

February 5, 1953 – Sweet rationing ends
Children throughout the country headed for their local sweet shops clutching their pocket money as unrationed sweets went on sale for the first time since the war. Toffee apples were the biggest sellers, with nougat and liquorice close behind. Grown-ups also joined in the sweet-buying frenzy, with workers queueing in their lunch hours for their favourite sweet treats.

Home hints

After a busy couple of months give your fridge a thorough clean. Start by washing the shelves and drawers in warm soapy water. Wipe down surfaces inside with an antibacterial spray and remember the door handle, too. Occasionally, vacuum the cooling elements to improve your fridge's efficiency.

Wise words

"What's fae you will not go by you"
My late mother-in-law used to say this (in a lowlands Scottish accent). Her reassurance, that if opportunities are meant to be you won't miss out on them, has really helped me in times of adversity and self-doubt.

Lin Kolatorowicz, Ballantrae

Headgear of yesteryear

This is my mum, Ivy Bradford, when she was 19 in the Twenties. I don't remember her wearing many hats after I was born, but I love this one! Of course, people didn't have their own cameras then so often had professional photos such as this taken. I think she was in service at the time, as a cook or chambermaid, perhaps. Shortly after this was taken she contracted rheumatic fever.

Rita Naylor, Sheffield, South Yorkshire

Recipe of the week

Spicy Chorizo, Pancetta & Bean Stew

Serves: 4–6
Preparation time: 15 minutes
Cooking time: 45 minutes

4 tbsp olive oil
1 small onion, finely diced
2 cloves garlic, crushed
2 tbsp tomato purée
125ml (4 ½fl.oz) red wine
2 tbsp sherry vinegar
2 tbsp caster sugar
2 tins plum tomatoes, roughly chopped (keeping the sauce)
1 medium chilli, thinly sliced
½ tsp smoked paprika
1 Bisto Beef Stock Melt
200g (7oz) cooking chorizo, sliced
200g (7oz) pancetta, diced
1 tin cannellini beans, drained and washed
2 tbsp fresh basil, chopped
Cracked black pepper

1. Gently fry the onion and garlic in oil until soft. Add the tomato purée and continue to fry for 2 minutes.
2. Add the red wine, sherry vinegar and sugar and boil for a further 2 minutes.
3. Add the chopped plum tomatoes, chilli, smoked paprika and the Bisto Beef Stock Melt and bring to the boil, then turn down the heat and simmer, stirring occasionally.
4. Meanwhile, fry the chorizo and pancetta in a little oil over moderate heat until coloured, then pass through a sieve to discard the fat. Add to the sauce. Simmer, with lid on, for 20 minutes. Add beans and simmer for a further 15 minutes.
5. Season to taste and stir through basil before serving.

© Bisto, www.facebook.com/AahBisto

10 Monday

11 Tuesday

12 Wednesday

13 Thursday

14 Friday

15 Saturday

16 Sunday

Every picture tells a story

Greta Garbo
Swedish actress

LN-NOM

Always a high flyer

My husband took this photo of Greta Garbo depicted on the wing of a Norwegian aeroplane. When I was in my early twenties, I was always impressed by Garbo's clear, fresh looks. I thought she had the most amazing features. She was described as an enigma and many people have tried to analyse her appeal but with little success. She was a mystery – and that was her appeal.

It is believed that she resisted appearing in 'talkies' for as long as she could as she feared her fans would lose interest when they heard her voice. The opposite happened – filmgoers were even more captivated by her softly spoken voice. I particularly loved the sound of her laugh which sounded strange and far away, and her boyish walk.

Hers was a timeless beauty. I think she would have been very happy to be still remembered, especially in such a spectacular fashion as in this image.

Margaret Turner, Warrington

On this week...

February 13, 1978 – Anna Ford reads the news
Anna Ford became ITV's first female newsreader when she joined ITN as their answer to the BBC's Angela Rippon. ITN newsreader Reginald Bosanquet welcomed her appointment saying: "I have never been averse to working with ladies." The former Tomorrow's World presenter moved to ITV's flagship News at Ten and stayed there until 1981.

Home hints

Fed up with clutter everywhere? Place baskets around the house to keep magazines, paperwork and oddments together. Once a week clear the baskets and put things away. Place another at the bottom of the stairs to keep washing and things for upstairs tidy. Everyday dedicate 15 minutes to jobs that never get done such as wiping down the cupboards and filing paperwork.

Wise words

"Begin any fault-finding with a kiss. Neglect the world rather than each other. And never speak loudly to one another (unless the house is on fire)"
This marriage advice may be old (from 1908) but is still true today.   **Mary King, Middlesbrough**

Headgear of yesteryear

My Aunty Margaret was probably in her early 20s in this photograph. She was a nursing sister at Storthes Hall Mental Hospital in Kirkburton, Huddersfield, which is where this photo would have been taken. Once she married she became a farmer's wife, which is how I remember her, so seeing her in this guise is wonderful. I'd love to have heard more stories of her time as a nurse in those days.
Mary Stott, via email

Recipe of the week

Chocolate Fondue
Serves: 2
Preparation time: 5 minutes
Cooking time: 5 minutes

2 strips orange rind
Large pinch ground cinnamon
3 tbsp caster sugar
120ml (4fl.oz) water
150g (5oz) dark chocolate, broken into pieces
2 tbsp double cream, plus 1 tbsp to decorate
350g (12oz) mixed strawberries, raspberries and blueberries

1 Add the orange rind, cinnamon, sugar and water to a small saucepan and heat gently until the sugar has dissolved. Simmer for 3-4 minutes until syrupy and leave to cool for 10 minutes – or longer, for the flavours to develop.
2 Discard the orange rind and reheat the syrup. Remove from the heat, add the chocolate and leave until melted. Stir until smooth and mix in 2 tbsp cream until glossy. Reheat gently if needed.
3 Arrange the fruit on a plate with fondue skewers or small forks and pour the fondue sauce into a cup or fondue pot set over a burner. Decorate with an extra drizzle of cream and swirl with a skewer. Start dipping!

Top Tip: For a minted chocolate fondue, substitute the orange and cinnamon for 2 stems of fresh mint.
© Seasonal Berries, www.seasonalberries.co.uk

17 Monday

18 Tuesday

19 Wednesday

20 Thursday

21 Friday

22 Saturday

23 Sunday

Every picture tells a story

PIC: REX FEATURES

Those good old radio times

When I was five, in 1940, my mother and I were evacuated to Somerset where we lived in an old cottage with a farm worker and his wife, Mr and Mrs Crick. They had a radio, a large old-fashioned box that stood in one corner of the tiny sitting-room. It was fed by something called an accumulator.

This was a glass container holding some type of acid and when this acid was getting low it had to be taken three miles to the nearest village to be exchanged for a fresh one, so frequent listening was discouraged. Instead, my mother bought a portable radio which ran on batteries – a real luxury. Among our favourite programmes were Bandwagon with Arthur Askey and Richard (Stinker) Murdoch, Life with the Lyons (starring Ben Lyon and Bebe Daniels) and Itma (short for It's That Man Again). My secret thrill was hiding behind the sofa at bedtime so I could hear the Paul Temple mystery series which always gave me a good old scare!

Peggy Critchlow, Nantwich, Cheshire

On this week...

February 23, 1963 – Farmer shocks traffic wardens

Peter Hicks, a farmer from Sussex, was in custody waiting to hear if he faced prosecution for electrifying his vehicle to ward off traffic wardens. Mr Hicks was arrested after a policeman heard a suspicious ticking noise coming from his Land Rover and received a nasty electric shock on touching it. "Until somebody tells me what law I'm breaking I shall keep up my private war," said the defiant farmer.

Home hints

Static hair can be a problem during the colder months if your hair is quite dry. Use conditioner after every wash and avoid drying your hair on the hottest setting, which can dry it further. A quick fix is to lightly rub a tumble sheet over it – it helps stop static and tame flyaway ends. Your hair will smell lovely and fresh, too.

Wise words

"Just be yourself, people will accept you for what you are, not what you try to be"
My eldest son gave this sage advice to me when I was nervous about going to stay with him on campus when he graduated in 1977. I've never forgotten it and quoted it to others over the years.
Sylvia Bolt, Cardiff

Headgear of yesteryear

This picture was taken several years ago when my hubby, Edwin, and I were invited to a fancy dress party in Wimblington, Cambridgeshire. If my memory serves me right it was an Edwardian theme. We did not have a great deal of time to get the costumes as we got the invitation at short notice but we were quite pleased at this result. My dress wasn't the most comfortable when sitting down but I loved it. **Maria Rix, Hunstanton, Norfolk**

Recipe of the week

Salmon Fillets with Garlic, Herb and Citrus Butter

Serves: 4
Preparation time: 15 minutes
Cooking time: 8 minutes

4 skinless salmon fillets
2 tbsp olive oil
Salt and freshly ground pepper
For the butter
80g (3oz) butter, softened
Finely grated zest and juice of 1 lime
Finely grated zest and juice of 1 lemon
1 tsp chopped fresh parsley
1 tsp chopped fresh chives
2 garlic cloves, finely chopped
To serve
Seasonal vegetables

1 Mix all the ingredients together for the flavoured butter, apart from the juice of the lemon and lime. Once all the ingredients have been mixed, whisk in the lemon and lime juice until it has been incorporated (the butter must be soft, otherwise the juice won't properly mix).
2 Preheat the grill, then cook the salmon for 3-4 minutes per side, brushing with olive oil and seasoning with salt and pepper.
3 Brush the salmon with the flavoured butter and continue to cook for 1 minute on each side.
4 Leave to rest for 2-3 minutes, then brush the remainder of the butter over the fish. Serve with blanched or boiled seasonal vegetables.
© Kerrygold, www.kerrygold.co.uk

24 Monday

25 Tuesday

26 Wednesday

27 Thursday

28 Friday

1 Saturday

2 Sunday

Every picture tells a story

A full house

In the early Fifties my parents took out a mortgage on a three-bedroomed terraced house in Portsmouth. To make some extra money to pay the bills, my mother took in lodgers as well as any family members who needed accommodation.

My grandmother came to live with us and took up residence in the front room. Emily, the lady who used to lodge with her and help with the chores, moved in to our end bedroom. She had her own furniture and loads of boxes crammed with things she had collected over the years. Her room smelled of mothballs and soap.

When Mum let the other two bedrooms to lodgers, my parents and I slept in the living room, folding our beds up during the day. With so many people in the house, my favourite place in the summer was the garden and my father had his shed out there to escape to. Although our house was full to bursting point, it was also filled with love and laughter and I never felt unhappy or alone.

Valerie Reilly, Ashford, Surrey

Home hints

If you didn't plant your spring flowering bulbs out in autumn then you still have time to do them this month, but you might have to cheat and opt for pot grown bulbs. Leave them in tubs for a pretty patio display or move them straight into your garden once the weather warms up and the frosts stop.

Wise words

"Think carefully before you use the words 'always' or 'never'"
Many years ago my husband and I helped to run a children's holiday mission. One of our staunchest supporters, Mrs Austen, gave us this advice on maintaining a happy marriage. I've remembered it every time I've been tempted to say 'you always…' or 'you never…' and I'm pleased to say we celebrate our 40th anniversary this year. **Liz Platt, by email**

Headgear of yesteryear

This is a photo of my mother, Gladys May Cooper, with what look like two huge bird wings on her hat! It's certainly not the type of hat you would wear out shopping. Mum was born in 1891 and died in 1984. I think she would have been in her early 20s in this picture. Mum had three brothers, so as the only girl I imagine she loved dressing up in lovely decorative outfits like this.

Joan Herbert, Portishead, North Somerset

On this week...

February 24, 1955 – Britain shivers in big freeze
Freezing temperatures and snow brought Britain to a standstill with 70 roads blocked, and trains and planes grounded. The RAF worked flat out to drop food and medical supplies to isolated areas, and farmers feared for their sheep out in the fields. Icy conditions continued into March in the worst freeze to hit the country for 30 years.

Recipe of the week

Leek, Red Pepper and Cashew Nut Lasagne

Serves: 4-6
Preparation time: 40 minutes
Cooking time: 50-60 minutes

850ml (30fl.oz) semi-skimmed milk
50g (2oz) olive oil spread
50g (2oz) plain flour
1 bay leaf
60g (2 1/4oz) grated parmesan
1 tbsp olive oil
3 leeks, sliced
3 red peppers, cubed
300g (10 1/2oz) ricotta
12 lasagne sheets (ready to cook)
50g (2oz) cashew nuts, roughly chopped
1/2 tsp nutmeg powder
100g (31/2oz) grated mozzarella
Salt and pepper

1 Preheat the oven to 180°C/350°F/Gas Mark 4.
2 Place the milk, spread, flour and bay leaf in a saucepan, season, and whisk together over a medium heat continually until it comes to simmering point and has thickened. Turn the heat down low and allow the sauce to cook gently for 5 minutes. Then, stir in 50g (2oz) parmesan, remove the pan from the heat and discard the bay leaf.
3 Heat the olive oil in a large frying pan, add the leeks and red peppers and cook until softened (approximately 5 minutes). Transfer into a large bowl and stir in the ricotta and cashew nuts. Season with black pepper and a pinch of salt.
4 Assemble the lasagne by spreading one-quarter of the sauce into the bottom of the dish, then one-third of the leek mixture and place sheets of lasagne on top of this. Repeat the whole process, this time adding one-third of the grated mozzarella, then the lasagne sheets. Repeat again, finishing with a layer of pasta, the rest of the sauce and the remaining parmesan and mozzarella.
5 Bake for 50-60 minutes until the top is golden and bubbling.
© British Leeks, www.british-leeks.co.uk

3 Monday

4 Tuesday

5 Wednesday

6 Thursday

7 Friday

8 Saturday

9 Sunday

Every picture tells a story

PIC: REX FEATURES

The great and the good

There was never one single person who was a role model for me when I was young, but there were several that I wanted to be like. Two of them are well-known stars. Harpo Marx was one of these. I loved his films and very much wished I could have met him. I also admired Adam Faith – ever since I saw a picture of him in the TV Times sitting on a Norton motor bike. It was the way he was looking at the camera that did it for me!

Apparently, he went through a lot in his lifetime but always loved meeting his fans. Other people who were an inspiration to me were not famous. I will always remember two girls, Sandra and Jennifer, who were at school with me at Sidestrand Hall in Cromer. They had a real zest for life, keeping myself and other children at the boarding school happy when we missed our parents.

Pamela Gregson, Telford, Shropshire

Home hints

Ensure you get a good night's kip and make the most of National Bed Month by giving your bedroom a sleep makeover. Banish the TV and electronic equipment and remove any clocks. Clear clutter and ensure that only restful, calming colours are present. Remember to regularly turn your mattress and replace your bed roughly every seven years.

Wise words

"Buy good shoes and a good bed"
My mother-in law always extolled the virtues of spending your money in the right places, adding: "If you're not wearing one you'll be in the other."
Beryl Turner, Peterborough

Headgear of yesteryear

I am very proud of this hat as it is a genuine Stetson. I worked on a stand selling Western wear and instead of wages was given this hat. In the picture, taken some years ago, I was stewarding at a Western horse show but just why I was doing a Tommy Cooper impression I don't remember! I only wear my Stetson about once a year to the WES Championship Show but I just can't part with it.

Pat Wells, Malvern, Worcestershire

On this week...

March 7, 1965 – Goldie the eagle defies capture
Goldie the golden eagle, normally a resident of Regent's Park Zoo in London, was still on the loose after outsmarting all attempts to catch him. A crowd of around 1,000 watched as zookeepers, police and firefighters tried to catch the escapee in Regent's Park. Goldie was finally recaptured after 12 days when he became hungry. Deputy head keeper Joe McCorry lured him back with a dead rabbit tied to a rope.

Recipe of the week

Irish Boxty Pancakes

Makes: 14
Preparation time: 15 minutes
Cooking time: 30 minutes

450g (1lb) potatoes, peeled
4 spring onions, finely sliced
100g (3 ½oz) plain flour
1 tsp bicarbonate of soda
1 large egg, separated
100ml (3 ½fl.oz) buttermilk or natural yoghurt
Salt and freshly ground black pepper
A little oil for frying
To serve
Fried egg, grilled bacon and tomatoes

1 Cut the potatoes into even chunks then cook in a large pan of boiling salted water for 10-15 minutes or until tender. Drain well, return to the pan then mash until smooth.
2 Stir in the spring onions and leave to cool – spreading thinly on a plate makes this happen quicker! Place the potatoes in a large bowl, sift over the flour, bicarbonate of soda, egg yolk and buttermilk, beat well and add plenty of salt and pepper.
3 Whisk the egg white in a separate clean bowl, until it forms stiff peaks, then fold into the potato mixture.
4 Heat a large, non-stick frying pan until hot, drizzle a little oil over the centre and wipe around the pan with a piece of kitchen paper. Drop 3-4 spoonfuls of the mixture into the pan and cook over a medium heat for about 8 minutes, turning once until golden – don't cook over too high a heat or the outside will brown before the centre is cooked. Remove from the pan and keep warm. Repeat to make about 16 pancakes in total.
5 Serve hot with a fried egg, grilled bacon and tomato.
Top tip: If you like, make the pancakes ahead and place them on a baking tray. Reheat at 200°C/400°F/Gas Mark 6 for about 10 minutes before serving.
© British Lion Eggs, www.eggrecipes.co.uk

10 Monday

11 Tuesday

12 Wednesday

13 Thursday

14 Friday

15 Saturday

16 Sunday

Every picture tells a story

Carry on, nurse

In 1961, aged 16, I became a cadet nurse. We cadets wore a starched cotton overall in custard yellow and were the 'gofers' who had to scrub out the instrument sterilisers, but drop everything the minute we were called upon to take specimens to the laboratory (we were obliged to walk at top speed at all times). We made gauze swabs by hand and another job was to mop the quarry-tiled floors with Lysol.

During training proper, which started when we were aged 18, we would pore over our anatomy and physiology books at the end of a long day's slog on the ward. It was mandatory to live in the Nurses' Home so there were no married students in those days. We all worked long hours, 12-hour night duties, six on and three off, and split day shifts, which left little time for leisure.

Friendships made with fellow student nurses have lasted a lifetime – the sights we saw and the tasks we had to do bound us together.

Kathryn Ashcroft, Skelmersdale, Lancs

On this week...

March 12, 1969 – Paul McCartney weds
Beatle Paul McCartney married American photographer Linda Eastman in a civil ceremony in London. Police held back throngs of excited fans as the couple entered Marylebone Register Office by a side door. The bride wore a bright yellow coat while her husband-to-be wore a matching tie. Linda already had a six-year-old daughter, Heather, and the couple went on the have three more children, Mary, Stella and James.

Home hints

Plant out summer flowering bulbs, early veg and your early potatoes. You'll know they are ready when they have sprouted green shoots of around 5cm (2in). Avoid pale coloured shoots by making sure they get enough light and that conditions are not too warm when chitting. Also, cut the grass and start tackling weeds before they take hold.

Wise words

"Who, by worrying, can ever add a single hour to their life?" (Matthew ch 6, v 34)
I have the 'worry gene' – my mother had it and my daughter has it too. We seem to have the capacity to turn a minor concern into a major catastrophe. I do try to remember this and another bible verse from Matthew (ch 6, v 34); 'Do not worry about tomorrow, for tomorrow will have enough worries of its own'.
B Grace, by email

Headgear of yesteryear

This photo, snapped by a street photographer in 1950s London, shows my mum (on the right) and 'Aunt' Elsie, carrying a lovely handbag and wearing a very unusual hat! 'Aunt' Elsie was the chief millinery buyer for Jenners, a posh department store in Edinburgh, so I'm sure this would have been very much in fashion at the time. When she visited us she always brought delicious Jenners chocolates with her.
Eppie Gould-Davies, Malaga, Spain

Recipe of the week

Sticky Orange Glazed Baked Ham

Serves: 6-8
Preparation time: 15 minutes, plus soaking if necessary
Cooking time: 2 hours 30 minutes

3kg (6 $^1/_2$lb) unsmoked, uncooked ham
1 large onion, sliced
Approx. 10 cloves
For the glaze
150g (5 $^1/_4$oz) dark soft brown sugar
25ml (1fl.oz) sherry vinegar
Juice of 1 large orange
1 tbsp English mustard

1 Refer to pack instructions and if necessary soak the ham the night before.
2 Pre-heat oven to 180°C/350°F/Gas Mark 4.
3 Place the ham, skin-side up, in a deep roasting tin, adding enough water to cover the base of the tin. Scatter the orange slices around the ham and cover tightly with foil. Cook in the centre of the oven for 2 hours.
4 While the ham is cooking, mix the sugar, vinegar, orange juice and mustard.
5. When the ham has had 2 hours in the oven, take it out and turn up the heat to 220°C/425°F/Gas Mark 7.
6 Remove the foil, leave the ham until cool enough to handle, then pour away any liquid in the tin. Using a sharp knife, carefully cut away the skin to leave an even layer of fat. Use the tip of the knife to score the ham fat diagonally at 3cm (1in) intervals - first in one direction, then the other, to produce a diamond pattern. Liberally paint the glaze over the fat, then stud with the cloves at the points of the diamond shapes.
7 Roast the ham for 30 minutes until glazed and just beginning to char around the edges. Serve warm or cold.
© Whitworths, www.whitworths-sugar.co.uk

17 Monday

18 Tuesday

19 Wednesday

20 Thursday

21 Friday

22 Saturday

23 Sunday

Every picture tells a story

A good read

My Grandma Ollier looked like a careworn Queen Victoria. Small and round, with a face criss-crossed with lines, when she laughed she showed teeth like half-peeled Brazil nuts. She lived in Crewe, in Hope Street, a curious name for a road with such a depressing appearance. As she had had eight children, Grandma Ollier had numerous grandchildren so there was nothing special about us. She treated us all with an indifference born of weariness. However, she was a great reader.

For tuppence a week she could borrow a book from the small library set up in the sweet shop at the end of the street. A penny was given back on the book's safe return. With a large magnifying glass, Grandma would sit at her oilcloth-covered table and read far into the night. When Auntie Agnes bought a radio, Grandma would shuffle next door to give the same concentration to a Shakespeare play on the BBC or comedians Elsie and Doris Waters.

Joyce Mansell, Chester, Cheshire

On this week...

March 20, 1952 – Bogey wins on Oscar
Humphrey Bogart won the only Oscar of his career for his portrayal of a gin-swilling riverboat owner in the hit film The African Queen. The script was originally written for a thick Cockney accent but had to be re-written because Bogart was not able to reproduce it. While his co-star, Katherine Hepburn, was very ill during filming, Bogart stayed well mainly, it's said, because he stuck to whisky rather than the local water.

Home hints

Fight sugar cravings with bitter tasting foods such as Radicchio. According to Chinese medicine, sugar cravings can be a symptom of an imbalance, which can be readdressed with bitter-tasting foods, such as the leaves of the chicory plant. As a bonus these foods are packed with B vitamins, which are also thought to help stop cravings.

Wise words

"All things will pass"
Many years ago I went through a very bad patch, sinking deep into depression. My wonderful mother took care of me and I remember her cuddles and her saying, 'It will pass, it will pass'. Now, when I find myself getting anxious or stressed, I whisper these simple words to myself and it really helps.

Kym Wheeler, Corby

Headgear of yesteryear

This is me with my baby son, Paul and my mother in about 1968, in front of our bungalow in Dorset. My hat was in the 'Beatles style' and it was bright pink with large white spots on it! Horrifying to think of it now but I felt rather 'cool' at the time. I married when I was 19 but didn't have Paul until I was 34, and memories of this time are very special to me.

Margaret Francis, Chester, Cheshire

Recipe of the week

St. Patrick's Day Cupcakes

Makes: 12
Preparation time: 20 minutes
Cooking time: 20-25 minutes

100g (3 $^{1}/_{2}$oz) butter
100ml (3 $^{1}/_{2}$fl.oz) stout
40g (1 $^{3}/_{4}$oz) cocoa powder
150g (5 $^{1}/_{4}$oz) plain flour
$^{1}/_{2}$ tsp salt
1 tsp baking powder
200g (7oz) light soft brown sugar
1 egg
75ml (3fl.oz) sour cream
For the frosting
200g (7oz) butter
450g (1lb) icing sugar, sifted
3-4 tbsp Irish cream liqueur
Green sugar sprinkles, to decorate

1 Preheat the oven to 180°C/350°F/Gas Mark 4. Line a 12-cup muffin tin with paper cases. Place the butter, stout and cocoa powder in a saucepan and place over a gentle heat, stir until the butter has melted and the mixture is smooth. Remove from the heat and allow to cool.
2 In a large bowl sift together the flour, salt, baking powder and sugar. Add the cooled stout mixture and beat for 1 minute using an electric whisk on a medium speed. Add the egg and sour cream and beat for a further 2 minutes.
3 Divide the batter evenly between the prepared tin. Bake for 20-25 minutes until cooked through and springy to the touch. Transfer the cakes to a cooling rack and leave to cool completely.
4 For the frosting, cream the butter in a bowl until light and fluffy. Gradually mix in the icing sugar a little at a time then beat in the Irish cream liquor. Spoon or pipe the icing on the cooled cakes and top with green sugar sprinkles to decorate.
© Kerrygold, www.kerrygold.co.uk

24 Monday

25 Tuesday

26 Wednesday

27 Thursday

28 Friday

29 Saturday

30 Sunday

Every picture tells a story

Beryl's dreamboat

I love narrow boats, but I had given up hope of ever travelling in one until the day my son came home on a visit. He said he had decided to take a narrow boat for a week. Overjoyed, I couldn't believe it. One morning in April, we set off. Our boat was called Lady Carol.

She was 62 feet long, plain outside but beautiful inside, with all mod cons including central heating. On the first evening, we struggled along a muddy footpath in the rain to eat in a riverside pub. The next morning was sunny so I sat out on the bow seat.

I was in heaven as we made our way up the Shropshire canal to Market Drayton. Cruising through the long Hardcastle tunnel was quite an experience. We negotiated our way through locks and met other friendly boat people. At some moorings the bank was low down and as I am a mere 4 foot 10 inches I had to jump into my son's arms so he could lift me to the bank. We fell about in fits of laughter.

Beryl M Bennett, Harworth, Doncaster

On this week...

March 25, 1950 – Ski-jumping on Hampstead Heath
Visitors to Hampstead Heath in north London were greeted to the sight of a full-size ski jump complete with snow and skiers. The snow, and most of the skiers, were from Norway. A team of 25 Norwegian skiers had brought the snow with them from their home country. There were 45 tons of it in all, and it had been transported packed in wooden boxes insulated by dry ice.

Home hints

Tackle pen ink stains on fabric with these methods. Lay the item on a white cloth and dab with surgical spirit then blot with a cloth. Keep doing this until the stain lightens and disappears. Soak the fabric and wash as normal. You could try soaking overnight in milk, spraying with hairspray before washing or have a go with nail varnish remover. Remember to always test the solution on an inconspicuous area beforehand though.

Wise words

"Count what you've got and not what you've not got"

My father had a difficult childhood – the youngest of six children, he was only seven when his father was killed in the First World War and his Mum died a few years later. When we were children if we moaned about our lot he'd simply remind us to be grateful for what we have.   **Liz Dally, by email**

Headgear of yesteryear

This is a photo of myself, aged 15, wearing a black beret style hat with trimming on the side. The two-piece suit I wore with it was also black and I wore it with a red blouse. I had been working in a solicitor's office for just under a year and clothing coupons were still around as it was 1945. The photo was taken at Polyfoto, where you got a sheet of pictures to choose from.

Eileen Vaughan, Lewes, East Sussex

Recipe of the week

Coconut and White Chocolate Macaroons

Makes: 16–18
Preparation time: 10 minutes
Cooking time: 15 minutes

2 large egg whites
$^1/_2$ tsp cream of tartar
100g (3 $^1/_2$oz fine caster sugar)
Pinch salt
250g (9oz) desiccated coconut
150g (5 $^1/_4$oz) white chocolate chips

1 Preheat the oven to 150°C/300°F/Gas Mark 2 and line a baking sheet with baking paper.
2 Beat the egg whites in a large bowl until frothy, add the cream of tartar and continue to beat until soft peaks are formed.
3 Add the sugar, 1 tsp at a time until it has all been incorporated and the meringue forms soft peaks.
4 Add half the chocolate chips and the remaining ingredients and mix thoroughly to combine.
5 Spoon 8 pyramids onto the baking tray, and bake for 15 minutes until lightly golden.
6 Cool on the tray for 2 minutes before transferring to a cooling rack.
7 Melt the remaining chocolate chips and drizzle over.
Top tip: The cream of tartar is not essential, but it does help to stabilise the egg white.
© Whitworths, www.whitworths-sugar.co.uk

31 Monday

1 Tuesday

2 Wednesday

3 Thursday

4 Friday

5 Saturday

6 Sunday

Every picture tells a story

Our family on film

When I was aged 13 in 1949, the house we lived in, Chapel House in Lordshill, Shropshire, was used as a location for the Powell and Pressburger film Gone to Earth. My grandparents, William and Jane Evans, were the caretakers of the chapel and our family lived there with them. My father had the job of recruiting around 100 extras from the nearby village of Snailbeach. I featured briefly in two scenes – the garden fête and dancing round the maypole.

I really loved my outfit of a long pink dress with a wide sash and a straw bonnet with a pink rose on it. We drank rather a lot of lemonade that day as the scene was shot over and over again to get it right. My mother had quite an important role as she was chosen to help the star of the film, Jennifer Jones (pictured above), down into the water in the baptism scene. She also appeared in the wedding breakfast scene which was shot at Shepperton studios.

Sylvia Lewis, Shrewsbury, Shropshire

On this week...

April 1, 1957 – BBC TV's spaghetti spoof
The BBC had the nation fooled with its spoof documentary about spaghetti crops in Switzerland. Narrated by the distinguished broadcaster Richard Dimbleby, the hoax Panorama programme claimed to show a Swiss family bringing in their annual spring spaghetti harvest. Some viewers were unimpressed by the BBC's hoax, but others wanted to know where they could get their own spaghetti bush.

Home hints

Get outdoors and get fit by enjoying a nice walk. Research shows that regular walking can reduce the risk of diabetes and heart disease. We should all aim to walk 10,000 steps a day, but build up to this gradually and go at your own pace. If you have a dog or can borrow a friend or neighbour's, experts reckon that they are just the motivation we need to keep it up.

Wise words

"Take care as you have a fortune in your health"
Times were hard in the Thirties but my dad understood more than most the true value of good health. He was injured in the First World War and suffered with asthma and bronchitis, but he was a very patient man and a good listener.

Irene Hickson, Christchurch

Headgear of yesteryear

This is a photo of myself, eight months pregnant, in 1962 at my brother-in-law's wedding. The heavy cotton suit, white with black design, was made for me by a friend. The skirt tied at the waist with tape, as it had a large circular hole in the front of it to accommodate the bump. Under the skirt I wore an 'apron' of the same material to fill in the hole. My hat was red to draw attention away from my bump!

Doreen Wyatt, Gravesend, Kent

Recipe of the week

Crusted Rack of Spring Lamb

Serves: 6
Preparation time: 30–40 minutes
Cooking time: 40 minutes

2 garlic cloves
50g (2oz) sun-dried tomatoes
3 tbsp wholeberry cranberry sauce
2 tsp fresh thyme leaves
Salt and freshly ground black pepper
3 racks of lamb (6 cutlets on each), chined

For the gravy
1 garlic clove, crushed
1 bottle rosé wine
1 large sprig fresh thyme
4 tbsp wholeberry cranberry sauce
2 tsp caster sugar
25g (1oz) butter

To serve
Creamy mash and green beans

1. To make the gravy: put the garlic, wine and thyme into a large pan, bring to the boil and boil rapidly for 15 minutes until reduced by half. Strain, discard the thyme and return the wine to the pan. Add the cranberry sauce and caster sugar and stir over a low heat until the sugar has dissolved. Set aside.
2. Preheat the oven to 200°C/400°F/Gas mark 6 Put the garlic, tomatoes, cranberry sauce and thyme into a processor and whizz to a smooth paste. Season well.
3. Trim most of the fat from the lamb. Spread the cranberry mixture evenly onto the outer side of the lamb. Put crust side up into a roasting tin and roast in the middle of the oven (20 minutes for medium–rare or 30 minutes for well done), covering the crust of the lamb loosely with foil if it starts to burn.
4. Transfer to a warm plate and leave to rest in a warm place for 5 minutes. Meanwhile, pour the wine mixture into the roasting tin and bring to the boil, scraping the pan juices into the gravy. Whisk in the butter until glossy. Season to taste.
5. Serve with gravy, creamy mashed potatoes and fine green beans.

© Ocean Spray, www.oceanspray.co.uk

7 Monday

8 Tuesday

9 Wednesday

10 Thursday

11 Friday

12 Saturday

13 Sunday

Every picture tells a story

Glam rock lives!

I had it all in 1973 – a feather-cut hairstyle, flared denims, cheesecloth shirts and a pair of boots (but the heels were only two inches high, not like the silver ones with five-inch heels that my heroine Suzi Quatro wore).

I spent all my spare money on seven-inch singles which I played on my first stereo record player. My bedroom walls were covered with posters of my favourite glam-rock stars – Slade, Sweet and Mud. In 1980, I finally got to see Suzi at the Hammersmith Apollo. That was the day I decided to learn to play the bass guitar, just like Suzi. I became good enough to form a band of my own.

Since then, I've been fortunate enough to see every band I worshipped back in those days. My love for glam has never wavered. And Suzi? We have become friends, I've been to hundreds of her gigs, and run her worldwide fan club. I'm still playing in my own band today and of course we play lots of Seventies music!

Lynn Chapman, Kingswood, Kent

Home hints

Enjoy avocado, which is rich in vitamins E and C. Give your skin a treat with this homemade facemask. Mash up a ripened avocado and mix with a teaspoon of honey (runny is best). Mix well and apply to the face, leaving for ten minutes. Rinse and your skin will feel instantly softer and more hydrated.

Wise words

"Always pull together – if you pull in opposite directions that's the way you'll go"
An elderly relative gave this advice to me just before our wedding day. I'm pleased to say it obviously worked because we celebrate our golden wedding anniversary this year – and we're still 'pulling together'.   **Ivy Jameson, Kempston**

Headgear of yesteryear

I am on the right of this photo, with my friend Jean on the left. We were born in the houses next door to each other and neither of us had any siblings, so we were always together. This shows us in Jean's back garden when I was four and Jean was three years old, when summers really were summer! I think my hat was blue and pink. We are still great friends 68 years on.   **Meryl Wood, Chirk, Wrexham**

On this week...

April 9, 1959 – NASA announces first astronauts
The first seven men selected for space travel included John Glenn, who became the first American to orbit the earth and Alan Shepard, the first American in space. The men were all highly trained test pilots and had been chosen to take part in Project Mercury, set to launch in 1961. The seven men became known as the Mercury Seven and were selected for their superb physiques and genius IQs.

Recipe of the week

Cappuccino Caramel Torte

Serves: 10-12
Preparation time: 45 minutes
Cooking time: 45-55 minutes

225g (8oz) unsalted butter, softened
225g (8oz) light muscovado sugar
200g (7oz) self-raising flour
25g (1oz) ground almonds
1 tsp baking powder
4 large eggs
1 tbsp instant coffee
For the caramel cream
300ml (10 ½fl.oz) double cream
250g (9oz) confiture de caramel
To decorate
White chocolate shards
Mini Easter eggs

1 Line a deep round cake tin with baking parchment. Preheat the oven to 180°C/350°F/Gas Mark 4.
2 Beat all cake ingredients except the coffee in a large bowl, until very smooth and creamy. Dissolve the coffee in 1 tbsp boiling water and blend in.
3 Spoon into the tin and bake for 45-55 minutes, until golden and firm. A skewer should come out clean. Cover loosely with foil if it browns early, and cool before turning onto a wire rack.
4 Meanwhile, whip the double cream until it just begins to thicken and hold its shape. The whisk will leave a trail when lifted. Add 2 tbsp confiture de caramel. Whisk back to the same consistency. Repeat until all the caramel has been incorporated and the cream forms soft peaks. Divide between two bowls.
5 Cut the cake in half, then half again to give four rounds. Use the first bowl of cream as filling between the rounds of cake, then spread the remainder over the top and sides. Decorate with white chocolate shards and mini Easter eggs.
© Bonne Maman, www.lovebonnemaman.co.uk

14 Monday

15 Tuesday

16 Wednesday

17 Thursday

18 Friday

19 Saturday

20 Sunday

Every picture tells a story

A very special dad

In this photo of hop picking in Kent my Father, Charlie Carter, is the little boy on the right with the frayed cap. Next to him is his sister, Jessie, who brought him and his two brothers up after their mum (also in the photo) died when Jessie was only 15.

They all thought the world of their big sister because if she hadn't taken on the role of 'mum', the family would have been split up and the boys would probably have gone into the workhouse. They lived in Canning Town in London.

To help earn some extra money, when he was a teenager my dad used to get wooden fruit boxes from the market, chop them up and sell them as kindling for the fire. When the war came, he joined the Royal Marines and was taken prisoner by the Japanese.

I remember him as a loving, hard-working father to my brother and me and our two stepsisters. He used to say: "It's not what's on the outside that counts, it's what's on the inside that matters."

Sally Brown,
Banbury, Oxon

On this week...

April 16, 1964 – Great train robbers jailed
More than 300 years in jail were handed out to 12 men who stole £2.6m in used bank notes from a night train travelling between Glasgow and London. Handing down the sentences Mr Justice Edmund Davies said it would be 'positively evil' if he showed any leniency. Public sympathy was strongly against the robbers because of their violent mistreatment of the train's driver, Jack Mills.

Home hints

Treat yourself to a fool-proof fake tan. Exfoliate beforehand to remove dry skin. Apply moisturiser to the knees, elbows and feet. Wear gloves and blend well for an even finish. After, wipe excess tan of your knees and elbows. If you do notice any mistakes once dry, wipe with an alcohol free toner or lemon juice on cotton wool.

Wise words

"The man that you marry shouldn't be the man you can live with but the man you can't live without"

This is something my boss said to me when I was a teenager. It's good advice that others should also follow. It must have worked for me because we've been married for 61 years.

Hazel Roberts,
Southport

Headgear of yesteryear

Some years ago I did voluntary work in a charity shop in Bearwood Road, Warley, West Midlands. This photo of the volunteer staff, taken about 15 years ago, shows us wearing our 'Easter bonnets', which were old straw hats donated during the winter and decorated with artificial flowers. I really enjoyed myself restoring those hats, which were snapped up at £5 each. I'm top left in the picture – I wonder where the other 'models' are now?

Brenda Wilkes,
Dereham, Norfolk

Recipe of the week

Hot Cross Buns

Makes: 12
Preparation time: 35 minutes
Cooking time: 2 hours

450g (1lb) strong white bread flour
1 tsp salt
2 tsp mixed spice
100g (3 1/2oz) caster sugar
7g (1/4oz) easy-blend dried yeast
250g (9oz) dried mixed fruit
50g (2oz) butter
250ml (9fl.oz) milk plus 3 tbsp
1 large egg, beaten
50g (2oz) plain flour
6 tbsp water

1 Sift the flour, salt, spice and 50g (2oz) sugar into a large bowl. Stir in the yeast and fruit. In a small pan, melt the butter, then add the milk and warm through. Stir into the dry ingredients with the egg and mix to form dough.
2 Knead for 10 minutes on a floured surface until smooth and elastic. Divide into 12 equal pieces and shape into balls. Place on a greased baking sheet, cover with oiled cling film and leave to prove in a warm place until doubled in size.
3 Preheat the oven to 190°C/375°F/Gas Mark 5. To make the crosses, mix the plain flour with the water. Spoon into a piping bag and neatly pipe a cross over each bun. Bake for 20-25mins, until golden brown.
4 For glaze, heat the remaining sugar and milk with 3 tbsp water in a small pan, stirring until dissolved. Boil for 1 min. Remove the buns from the oven and brush twice with glaze. Leave to cool on a wire rack.

© British Lion Eggs, www.eggrecipes.co.uk

21 Monday

22 Tuesday

23 Wednesday

24 Thursday

25 Friday

26 Saturday

27 Sunday

Every picture tells a story

Haymaking in Mill Hill

My father and his brother were the tenants of Rosebank Farm in Mill Hill. In this photo our two families are taking a break from haymaking – I am the middle little girl perched on the bonnet with my Auntie Phoebe and that's my brother and uncle in front, leaning on their pitchforks.

It was hard work and long hours, but what fun we had. My cousin, Jean, says some of the tales we could tell would be even more eccentric than The Darling Buds of May. If an animal wasn't well, Auntie Phoebe would bring it indoors and it wasn't unusual to find goats in the bathroom or even a donkey in the bedroom.

We never had a bank account so the money we made from selling our produce or rearing turkeys for Christmas was simply stuffed away in drawers. We once had a disaster when my father allowed four tramps to spend the night in one of the barns. To keep warm, they lit a fire which spread rapidly and required nine fire engines to extinguish it.

Gill Ball, Kislingbury, Northants

On this week...

April 24, 1981 – IBM launches first home computer
The small size of the 5150 IBM Personal Computer and its relatively low price of $1,565 made it an instant success with the public. It was so popular that, a year after its launch at New York's elegant Waldorf Astoria Hotel, Time magazine chose the computer as its 1982 'Man of the Year'. The humble 5150 PC only had a tiny fraction of today's computer memories, but singlehandedly sparked the home computing revolution.

Home hints

Whenever making any payments online remember to look for the secure padlock symbol in the top right hand corner of the security status bar and the 'S' for secure which will appear after the http in the address bar.

Wise words

"Babies need to get used to noise"
When I bought my son home from hospital 52 years ago a neighbour told me the best thing you can do is get him used to lots of noise. There was no, 'ssh the baby's asleep' in our house. Consequently he (and later my other two) would sleep through anything.

Enid Ewing, by email

Headgear of yesteryear

This is a photo of my lovely granddaughter Heidi who lives in Canberra, Australia with my son, daughter-in-law and two more granddaughters. This photo was taken on one of my rare visits to Australia when Heidi was seven years old. She asked me to help make a bonnet for her school's Easter parade. This is the result – Heidi particularly wanted the Easter chicks included! She is now 17 and studies at college in Canberra.

Sheila Margrie, Sunbury-on-Thames, Surrey

Recipe of the week

Savoury Dragon's Feet

Makes: 10
Preparation time: 50-60 minutes, including proving
Cooking time: 12-15 minutes

500g (1lb 1 ½oz) Wright's sunflower bread mix
3 tbsp sage and onion stuffing
1 medium egg
40g (1 ¾oz) butter
1 tbsp tomato puree
260ml (9fl.oz) warm water
1 medium egg, beaten, for wash

1 Mix all the ingredients to make up a well-developed dough.
2 Divide into 10 pieces and form into balls. Cover with a damp tea towel, lightly oiled cling film and rest for 5 minutes.
3 Mould each piece into an oval shape, flatten one side and cut to form 5 toes.
4 Place on a greased baking tray, cover again and prove in a warm place for 30–40 minutes or until doubled in size.
5 Egg wash and bake in a preheated oven at 230°C/450°F/Gas mark 8 for 12-15 minutes until golden brown.
© Wright's Home Baking, www.wrightsflour.co.uk

28 Monday

29 Tuesday

30 Wednesday

1 Thursday

2 Friday

3 Saturday

4 Sunday

Every picture tells a story

Queen of the May

I was brought up in the pretty village of Melmerbury in Cumbria where my parents had a small farm. In the photo my mother is pushing my brother Kenneth in the pram and I am walking alongside holding a bunch of wild flowers.

We had a very happy childhood and although we didn't have many toys we improvised games such as, seeing who could catch the most bumble bees in a jam jar or making mud pies in the little play house we had in a shed. My best friend was the blacksmith's daughter. We played safely on the village green where every May we children danced round the maypole.

When I was 13, it was my turn to be Queen of the May. The village green also served as the playground for the village school where I was taught by a wonderful headmistress, Miss Harding. She inspired me to become a teacher myself and we always kept in touch even when I moved away to live and work in London for many years.

Margaret Dixon, Penrith, Cumbria

On this week...

May 2, 1933 – First sighting of Nessie
Although reports of a mysterious creature living in Loch Ness date back centuries, the modern legend was born when the Inverness Courier reported that a local couple had seen 'an enormous animal rolling and plunging on the surface'. The story became a media phenomenon with London newspapers sending correspondents to Scotland, and a circus offering £20,000 for the monster's capture. To this day Nessie has eluded detection!

Home hints

Keep track of changeable weather with soaring temperatures and even the occasional late frost. Make sure you plan ahead and protect any young plants from the extremes. Start cutting your lawn regularly and now's a good time to repair any bare patches and give it a good feed. And, of course, weed, weed, weed!

Wise words

"Live each day as if it's your last"
My dad always taught us that life is short and you never know what's around the corner, that it's important to appreciate what you have and not take things for granted. I do try to keep his words in mind. **Nicola Hunt, Essex**

Headgear of yesteryear

This is me (on the left) wearing my tall, pale blue hat on the occasion of my brother's ordination to the priesthood. Soon afterwards I wore it when I travelled to Germany to become a teacher to the Forces' children. I made great friends, who later said they thought I was very stuck up because of my hat! I am now a hatless Grannie to ten, and my brother still serves his parish with great enthusiasm.

Pauline Barnes, Newburgh, Lancashire

Recipe of the week

Mini Passion Cakes

Serves: 16
Preparation time: 30 minutes
Cooking time: 20 minutes

500g (1lb 1oz) Wright's carrot cake mix
227g (8oz) crushed pineapple
(drained and juice reserved)
Reserved juice plus water, made up to 200ml (7fl.oz)
4 tbsp vegetable oil
50g (2oz) desiccated coconut
2 ripe bananas, mashed
For the filling
250g (8 3/4oz) mascarpone cheese
4 passion fruits
For the topping
100g (3 1/2oz) icing sugar
1 passion fruit

1 Place the cake mix, water and oil in a bowl and beat to form a smooth batter.
2 Add the pineapple, coconut and bananas and mix well.
3 Divide the mixture into 16 well-greased mini cake tins.
4 Bake in the lower half of a preheated oven at 180°C /360°F/Gas Mark 4 for 18-20 minutes, until firm to the touch.
5 Allow to cool in the tin before removing to a wire rack.
6 Scoop the pulp and the seeds from the passion fruit and mix with the mascarpone cheese to make the filling – then sandwich between two layers of cake (simply cut each mini cake in half).
7 For topping, scoop the seeds and pulp from the passion fruit and form a paste with the icing sugar, then drizzle over.
© Wright's Home Baking, www.wrightsflour.co.uk

5	Monday

6	Tuesday

7	Wednesday

8	Thursday

9	Friday

10	Saturday

11	Sunday

Every picture tells a story

What happened to Whitsun?

I remember when Whitsun was the prelude to summer – the day when we children could finally cast off our liberty bodices and thick black stockings and consign them to the airing cupboard until the following winter.

We set out for church on Sunday in let-down summer dresses, socks and sandals, enjoying the breeze on our legs, and prayed that Monday would be a fine day. The following morning we crowded on to three or four lorries which took us to a field where a large marquee had been erected.

The morning was spent playing games and exploring. Lunch was a thick white sandwich, a bun and a cup of milk. In the afternoon our parents arrived. Perched upright on wooden chairs, hats firmly tied to their heads with scarves, they watched the sack, egg-and-spoon and three-legged races. Going home, we hung precariously over the sides of the lorries, our faces burned red from the sun. No one had heard of health and safety – or sunscreen – in those far-off days.

Rhona Sheppard, Southampton

On this week...

May 6, 1994 – Channel tunnel opens
Queen Elizabeth II and French President Francois Mitterand opened a rail tunnel connecting Britain to the European mainland for the first time since the last Ice Age 8,000 year ago. Embarking at London and Paris respectively their trains met nose to nose at Calais where the ceremony took place. Running for 23 miles under water, the 'Chunnel' is still the world's longest under-sea tunnel.

Home hints

Eat rhubarb. Packed full of nutrients, rhubarb is an excellent source of immune-boosting vitamin C and also dietary fibre – important for maintaining healthy digestion. Research has found that it can help lower cholesterol and contains antioxidants, which have been linked to fighting cancer.

Wise words

"Work hard, it is a blessing to the soul"
At school in the Fifties our temporary English teacher, Mr Cooper, loved to hand out 'lines' as a punishment. I still vividly remember the words he told us to write, which ended with, 'No man is more to be pitied than he who has nothing to do'.

Morwyn Jones, Blackwood, Gwent

Headgear of yesteryear

Here I am at a garden fête in around 1963, blowing up this unusual balloon to amuse my baby, Claire. My family always supported the church in our little village, and this was a lovely event I attended with my mother and Claire, who was only a few months old. I have always loved hats, and this navy straw one was perfect for the occasion – especially as this photo ended up in our local paper!

Audrey Chatterton, Spilsby, Lincolnshire

Recipe of the week

Berry Crunch Breakfast
Serves: 4
Preparation time: 10 minutes

30g (1oz) desiccated coconut
3 tbsp almonds
3 tbsp hazelnuts
3 tbsp pumpkin seeds
1 tbsp ground flaxseed
200g (7oz) fresh blueberries or mixed berries
200g (7oz) Yeo Valley blueberry with a hint of lime yoghurt (or 200g (7oz) blueberry yoghurt and a dash of lime juice)

1 Lightly toast the desiccated coconut and nuts until golden brown. Allow to cool for a minute or two, then pop in a food processor or blender with the pumpkin seeds and pulse until coarsely chopped. Stir in the flaxseed.
2 Swirl the berries through the yoghurt.
3 Spoon into four glasses and top with the nut and seed mixture.

Top Tip: For a further flavour boost, add 1 tbsp crème de cassis to the berries!
© Yeo Valley, www.yeovalley.co.uk

12 Monday

13 Tuesday

14 Wednesday

15 Thursday

16 Friday

17 Saturday

18 Sunday

Every picture tells a story

A lesson for life

My role model was Mrs Roscoe, my primary school teacher. Although she had a club foot and had to wear a built-up shoe, she was very elegant and wore her dark hair in a bun.

She was a quiet lady – I never heard her shout – who knew how to get the best out of children. Mrs Roscoe was a great storyteller and had us all transfixed with tales of her son, Kenneth, who was away in the Navy.

One day she gathered us together and told us that her fountain pen, a present from Kenneth, had disappeared from her desk. She said: "You all know about Kenneth and he'd be so upset, as I am, about the loss of his gift to me. It would make us very happy if the pen was returned to my desk before we go home." It was, and no one was ever accused of the theft (although we had our suspicions).

I learned a lot from that experience about how to cope with difficult situations as well as the right and wrong way to handle people. Thank you, Mrs Roscoe.

Alice Schofield, Eccleshall, Staffs

On this week...

May 16, 1990 – Gummer's burger stunt
At the height of the panic about BSE in beef, Minister of Agriculture John Gummer attempted to reassure the British public by getting his daughter, Cordelia, to eat a beef burger in front of the press. When the four year old declined, he bit into the burger himself and declared it 'absolutely delicious'. In 1996, research revealed a link between BSE and the human form of the disease, CJD.

Home hints

Get your feet ready for sandals by painting your toenails a fresh summer shade. For a neater finish and to prevent your polish wandering onto your cuticles, dab Vaseline around your nail edge. Make sure the nail surface is Vaseline free, apply polish as normal and then, once dry, wipe away the Vaseline and any mistakes!

Wise words

"Always be on time"
Our headmaster always tried to drum into us how important it is to be punctual, by adding: "The worst words you can hear is 'Too late!'"

Mrs D Thompson, Fairford

Headgear of yesteryear

This photo was taken at a friend's wedding in 1960. I made the dress myself with a proper nylon underskirt, which was very scratchy but that was the fashion at the time. I didn't wear hats very often and was reluctant to buy one, so I borrowed this white one from a colleague. The style meant it just sat on the top of my head so it fitted perfectly, and was a pretty good match for the outfit.

Beryl Wood, Denton, Manchester

Recipe of the week

Cranberry & Goats' Cheese Salad

Serves: 4
Preparation time: 10 minutes
Cooking time: 5 minutes

400g (14oz) soft goats' cheese, rind trimmed
50g (2oz) dried cranberries
2 tbsp white wine vinegar
5 tbsp olive oil
1 tsp Dijon mustard
1 tsp herbes de provence
Pinch sugar
250g (8 ³/₄oz) mixed salad leaves
Sea salt and black pepper
Lemon rind, to garnish

1 Preheat the grill to a medium to high setting. In a bowl, mash the goats' cheese and work in the dried cranberries with a fork or your fingertips. Roll the cheese into walnut-sized balls and place on a baking sheet.
2 Grill the goats' cheese for a few minutes, until the surface is just starting to brown. Remove and set aside.
3 In a jar, mix together the vinegar, oil, herbs, mustard and sugar. Shake well and season to taste.
4 Toss the dressing over the salad leaves and pile into bowls. Top with the grilled goats' cheese and serve garnished with lemon rind.

© Ocean Spray, www.oceanspray.co.uk

19	Monday

20	Tuesday

21	Wednesday

22	Thursday

23	Friday

24	Saturday

25	Sunday

Every picture tells a story

Never such devoted sisters

Here I am on an early seaside holiday in Mablethorpe, flanked by my two older sisters, Pat (on the left) and Jan. Our family lived in Lincoln and went to Mablethorpe every year where we stayed in one of two cottages which were exotically called Shangri La and Beau Geste.

I was a late baby (probably rather a shock to my parents!) so my sisters were aged 15 and 12 when I was born. They were like mothers to me, fed me, bathed me, changed my nappies and also made my clothes. They were both clever needlewomen and had made the skirts they are wearing in the photo. Pat also knitted her smart Fair Isle top.

Many years later, Pat told me that when she took me out for a walk in my pram she used to slip a curtain ring on her finger so that people would not mistakenly assume I was her illegitimate baby! The three of us are still very close although when I was eight years old Jan married and went to live in America. **Gill Whitworth, Lincoln**

On this week...

May 24, 2010 – Lawnmower driver sets record
Lawnmower enthusiast Don Wales broke the world land speed record for a lawnmower twice in one weekend at Pendine Sands in Carmarthenshire. Wales landed a place in the Guinness World Records after racing his vehicle to speeds in excess of 87mph. Speed runs in Wales' family – he is grandson of Sir Malcolm Campbell, who broke the world land speed record at the same spot in 1924.

Home hints

Descale your kettle without needing to buy any fancy kits of cleaning products, by using vinegar. Simply fill your kettle with a solution of half water and half white vinegar. Leave overnight and then empty, wipe and rinse, before filling and re-boiling at least twice so it's thoroughly rinsed. Then sit back with a lovely cuppa and admire your hard work.

Wise words

"Save your tears for bigger sorrows"
As a little girl I often cried over things that seemed to me to be the end of the world. At such times my dad would put his arm around me and say these words. It's only now I'm older that I've come to really appreciate what he meant.

Jean Fisher, Leeds

Headgear of yesteryear

Our school, Pendleton High School for Girls in Salford, went on a visit to the Festival of Britain in 1951. This is a photo of a group of us older pupils outside our hotel. Summer school uniform had by now come to our school so younger girls all wore the striped dresses, but we older girls were allowed our own choice of dress. As you can see, berets or summer Panamas had to be worn at all times.

Joan Hamer, Salford, Lancashire

Recipe of the week

Posh Fridge Cake

Makes: 20 pieces
Preparation time: 20 minutes
Chilling time: 3 ½ hours

200g (7oz) dark chocolate, broken into pieces
50g (2oz) butter
2 tbsp golden syrup
175g (6oz) soft amaretti biscuits or good shortbread biscuits, roughly broken
50g (2oz) pistachio nuts, roughly chopped
175g (6oz) raspberries
150g (5oz) blueberries
75g (3oz) white chocolate, melted

1 Line a 20cm (8in) shallow, square cake tin with a large square of non-stick baking paper, snipping diagonally into the corners of the paper then pressing the paper into the tin so that the base and sides are lined.
2 Add the dark chocolate, butter and golden syrup to a bowl set over a pan of gently simmering water, and heat for about 5 minutes, stirring until the chocolate has melted and the mixture is smooth and glossy.
3 Take the bowl off the heat, add all the biscuits and, keeping a few nuts and berries back for the top, stir the rest into the chocolate mix. Spoon into the paper lined tin and press into an even layer. Sprinkle with the remaining nuts and fruit. Chill for 3 hours until firm.
4 To finish, drizzle the melted white chocolate over the top of the cake in zig-zag lines using a dessert spoon, then chill for an extra 30 minutes until set. Lift the cake out of the tin, peel away the paper and cut into small squares.

Top tip: Keep in the fridge and eat within 2 days.
© Seasonal Berries, www.seasonalberries.co.uk

26 Monday

27 Tuesday

28 Wednesday

29 Thursday

30 Friday

31 Saturday

1 Sunday

Every picture tells a story

My remarkable mother

My brothers nicknamed our mother The Matriarch because everyone, even our neighbours, went to her for help, advice and consolation. Her real name was Harriet Lilian and she was a rather plump lady with twinkling blue eyes.

When she was a child, she had spent eight years in an orphanage where she had received a basic education, but her aim in life was to learn as much as she could by reading. Her thirst for knowledge was unbelievable. I cannot imagine how she found time to keep up her self-education while working full-time and caring for a family of five children. Her first love was poetry and especially Shakespeare's plays from which she could quote long passages off by heart.

When she read to us and made up bedtime stories, she held us all spellbound. She wrote plays for us and the other children in our street and encouraged their mothers to make our costumes so we could act them out in our garden.

Mary Archer, via email

On this week...

May 28, 1959 – Monkeys in space
The United States sent a pair of monkeys, Able and Baker, into space on a Jupiter missile. They survived forces 38 times greater than gravity and were weightless for nine minutes during their 16-minute flight. Sadly Able died shortly after, but Baker lived a long and happy life at the US Space and Rocket Centre in Alabama until his death in 1984.

Home hints

Get ready for a garden of blooms. Now's the time to prune spring shrubs and deadhead roses regularly to encourage a longer flowering period. Harvest early vegetables including potatoes, radishes and salads and take cuttings from herbs such as rosemary and sage. Don't forget to water the pots and hanging baskets on warmer days.

Wise words

"Spend a little, save a little and waste a little"
When I left school and earned my first wage my mum passed on this advice that she, in turn, received from her mother. It may be very sensible to save for a rainy day but don't forget to enjoy yourself along the way.

Joan Bound, Farnborough

Headgear of yesteryear

This photo was taken in 1948 when I was 18 years old. My suit is powder blue, and I managed to get a bowler hat that matched the colour very well. The stitched sandals were the height of fashion, and I made the blouse myself from a scrap of pale pink satin. I was working as a magistrate's clerk at the time, and this is how we dressed on most occasions.

Elizabeth Atkinson, Draycott, Derbyshire

Recipe of the week

Asparagus, Watercress and Tomato Risotto

Serves: 4
Preparation time: 15 minutes
Cooking time: 30 minutes

4 tbsp olive oil
4 shallots, finely chopped
2 garlic cloves, sliced
2 bundles of asparagus, trimmed and cut into 3cm (1in) lengths
100g (3 $^1/_2$oz) red and yellow cherry tomatoes, cut in half
200g (7oz) risotto rice
1 small glass of white wine (usually 125ml / 4 $^1/_4$fl.oz)
1litre (1 $^3/_4$pt) hot vegetable stock
2 bunches of watercress, roughly chopped
50g (2oz) lightly salted butter, cut into cubes
50g (2oz) grated parmesan
Salt and cracked black pepper

1 In a large saucepan, heat 2 tablespoons of olive oil and then add the shallots and garlic. Sweat for 10 minutes until the shallots and garlic turn translucent without any colour.
2 While the shallots and garlic are cooking, heat a medium-sized frying pan, add the rest of the oil. When the oil starts to smoke add the asparagus and tomatoes. Season with salt and pepper, cook for 30 seconds or until the tomatoes start to wilt slightly, then remove from the heat and set aside.
3 By now the onions should be ready. Stir in the rice, and keep cooking and stirring until that has also turned translucent, then add the wine and simmer until it has reduced by half.
4 Now start to add the hot stock, stirring the rice every now and then. Keep adding the stock a little at a time until the rice is cooked with a slight bite to it (this should be about 20 minutes).
5 When the rice is cooked, stir in the watercress, asparagus and tomatoes. Remove from the heat and add the butter and half of the cheese. Season to taste.
6 Serve in warm bowls, sprinkled with the rest of the cheese.

© British Asparagus, www.british-asparagus.co.uk

June 2 - 8

2	Monday
3	Tuesday
4	Wednesday
5	Thursday
6	Friday
7	Saturday
8	Sunday

Every picture tells a story

PIC: REX FEATURES

Day trip to London

In 1953 when I was aged 11, we had a school trip to London to see the Coronation decorations. This was very exciting for us as we lived over 200 miles away in Cheshire and none of us had been to London before. My day started with a three-mile bike ride to the station to catch the 7.30am train which was full of noisy, excited schoolchildren.

I sat with my three best friends. None of us had a watch so we ate our packed lunches and discovered afterwards that it was only 9.30am! When we arrived we boarded an open-top double-decker bus for a sightseeing tour. Next we had a trip up the Thames on a cruise boat, then back on a bus for a visit to London Zoo to see the famous baby polar bear, Brumas.

We were given a special tea at the Zoo's café before leaving for the journey home. I eventually arrived back at 10pm. As it was summertime, it was still light, but my mother said she had never seen anyone look so tired as me!

Joyce Duffy, via email

On this week...

June 4, 1968 – Dover culls seagulls
The townspeople of Dover began their annual purge of their feathered co-habitants. Town leaders decided to take action after complaints about the gulls' noisy dawn chorus and soiling of cars and washing. Residents and workmen worked together to remove hundreds of nests and eggs. Some risked injury as anxious mother gulls dive-bombed workers trying to remove their eggs.

Home hints

Munch on asparagus while it's in season. This natural age-fighter is a good source of fibre, folate and vitamins A, C and E – all essential for your general wellbeing. Asparagus does perish quicker than other vegetables, so to keep it fresher for longer wrap the ends in damp kitchen paper and store in the fridge.

Wise words

"If a job's worth doing, it's worth doing well"
At the tender age of nine, when learning to knit and sew, my mother instilled in me a work ethic that's stayed with me. Mum died when I was 13 and I took over running the house. Later, in the Army, I was never sent back to re-iron my uniform! And in married life I worked to take care of my husband and four sons.   **Rosemary Niblett, Stoke on Trent**

Headgear of yesteryear

We had a super street party to celebrate the Queen's Silver Jubilee in 1977, with a fancy hat parade for the children. This is my daughter Ruth wearing a hat made by me, with silver tin foil (which always came in handy in those days!) and lots of flags. Ruth, who was ten at the time, was reluctant to wear the hat because it was so big, but we were both pleased when we won first prize!
          Pat Rose, Sidmouth, Devon

Recipe of the week

Sizzling Chilli and Peach Chicken

Serves: 4
Preparation time: 20 minutes
Cooking time: 20 minutes

50g (2oz) palm or dark muscovado sugar
1 tsp ground turmeric
1 red chilli, deseeded and finely shredded
5cm (2in) piece fresh ginger, peeled and finely grated
3 tbsp fish sauce
Juice of 2 limes
4 tbsp peach conserve
8 boned chicken thighs, skin on
2 tbsp rapeseed oil
3 fat garlic cloves, sliced
To finish
Shredded spring onion
Fresh mint
Chopped salted peanuts
1 lime, quartered

1 Put the sugar, turmeric and 3 tbsp water in a small saucepan and heat slowly, stirring, for 2–3 minutes until the sugar has dissolved.
2 Add the chilli, ginger, fish sauce, lime juice and conserve. Increase the heat and bubble for 1–2 minutes until a deep, golden caramel brown. Remove from heat.
3 Cut the chicken into large, bite-sized pieces. Heat the oil in a wok or large frying pan and fry the chicken with the garlic for 3–4 minutes, until golden brown and crisp.
4 Pour in half the chilli peach caramel and let it bubble up and sizzle for 2–3 minutes.
5 Sprinkle with spring onions, mint and peanuts, squeeze over a little lime and serve immediately. Offer the remaining chilli peach caramel separately.

Top Tip: Delicious served cold with salad, or cut the hot chicken into fine shreds and serve in bread wraps with soured cream and salad leaves
Extra Top Tip: Instead of chicken, try with 450g (1lb) raw king prawns!
© Bonne Maman, www.lovebonnemaman.co.uk

9 Monday

10 Tuesday

11 Wednesday

12 Thursday

13 Friday

14 Saturday

15 Sunday

Every picture tells a story

Beside the seaside

This is me aged two, sitting on Ramsgate beach wearing a pink outfit knitted by my mum. Just after this photo was taken I fell forward into the hole I was digging and even after 70 years I can still remember the horrible taste of the gritty sand in my mouth.

Ugh! My dad quickly bought me an ice cream to help dry my tears. We lived in Morden in Surrey and had a seaside holiday every year, usually in Ramsgate, but we also went to Bournemouth or Brighton.

It was on the prom at one of these resorts that my sister Brenda and I had our photo taken with a huge stuffed tiger. As my parents never owned a car, we always travelled by train, and stayed in a guest house.

One year, my mum was horrified when we went into the guesthouse dining room to find a sticky fly catcher hanging from the ceiling, covered in dead flies. She said: "Oh George, we're not going to stay here again!"

Pat Rose, Sidmouth, Devon

Home hints

Freshen up a pongy dustbin with a sprinkle of bicarbonate soda. Wipe down your kitchen bin inside and out regularly to stop bad smells and germs building up. A solution of water and vinegar is perfect for this. Then sprinkle in some bicarbonate soda, leave to soak for a few minutes before rinsing with warm water.

Wise words

"Keep a week's wages in hand"
Just before we got married in the Fifties my Granny gave me £5 (the equivalent of my husband-to-be's weekly wage) so we would always have a week's money in case of emergencies. She also said: "Never borrow, if you want it badly enough save up and give something up."

Jennifer Hochrath, Rothwell

Headgear of yesteryear

It was June 1960 and I was meeting my boyfriend's parents for the first time. I chose a black blazer, white pleated skirt and white accessories, topping it off with a straw boater, or a cadie as we called them in Lancashire. I had quite a distance to travel, and was so proud of the stares I had standing at bus stops! We have now been married for 50 years, and often speak of this day.

Jacqueline Warburton, Bradford, West Yorkshire

On this week...

June 10, 1977 – Greedy fish finally caught
After two years of helping itself to goldfish in trawler captain Alf Leggett's fish-breeding pond, a killer perch was finally outwitted by two men from the local water board. Nicknamed Jaws, the greedy perch had eaten around 3,000 goldfish by the time it was caught. The men from the water board used a stun rod to daze the perch before scooping it up with a large net.

Recipe of the week

Chocolate and Raspberry Tart

Serves: 8
Preparation time: 30 minutes, plus 30 minutes chilling
Cooking time: 40–50 minutes, plus 1 hour cooling

For the pastry
175g (6oz) plain flour
15g ($\frac{1}{2}$oz) cocoa powder
50g (2oz) caster sugar
100g (3 $\frac{1}{2}$oz) butter, diced
2 egg yolks

For the filling
250ml (8fl.oz) double cream
125ml (4fl.oz) semi skimmed milk
150g (5oz) dark chocolate, broken into pieces
2 medium eggs
65g (2 $\frac{1}{2}$oz) caster sugar
$\frac{1}{2}$ tsp vanilla extract
175g (6oz) fresh raspberries

To decorate
Extra raspberries and cocoa powder

1 Sift the flour and cocoa into a bowl, add the sugar and rub the butter in with fingertips to make fine crumbs. Stir in the egg yolks and bring together to form a ball. Add a little cold water if needed.
2 Knead and roll out to line a 24cm (9$\frac{1}{2}$in) flan tin, 2.5cm (1in) deep. Ease the pastry into the flutes, leaving a little extra to allow for shrinkage during baking. Prick and chill for 30 minutes.
3 Preheat oven to 190°C/375°F/Gas Mark 5. Line the pastry with baking paper and baking beans. Cook for 10 minutes. Remove paper and beans then cook for another 5-10 minutes until crisp.
4 Meanwhile, pour the cream and milk into a pan, bring just to the boil, remove from heat and add the chocolate. Leave until melted. Whisk the eggs, sugar and vanilla together until smooth, then gradually whisk into the chocolate milk.
5 Sprinkle raspberries over the base of the pastry case. Strain the chocolate over and cook at 160°C/325°F/ Gas Mark 3 for 25-30 minutes, or until just set.
6 Leave to cool at room temperature for at least an hour. Decorate with extra raspberries and sifted cocoa before serving.
© Seasonal Berries, www.seasonalberries.co.uk

June 16 - 22

16 Monday

17 Tuesday

18 Wednesday

19 Thursday

20 Friday

21 Saturday

22 Sunday

Every picture tells a story

Variety was the spice of life

I still love a night out at the theatre but I sadly miss the variety shows that I used to see with my mother. Every Friday we would join the queue for first house at The Lyceum theatre in Crewe.

We always sat in the same seats, right at the back of the stalls. I adored the atmosphere and the red and gold decor. The tap of the orchestra conductor's baton on the stand was the signal for the curtains to sweep back, revealing a row of smiling high-kicking chorus girls.

They were followed by all sorts of acts from trapeze artists to performing dogs and singers – I remember a young Julie Andrews singing Ave Maria, followed by her parents singing a selection from The Desert Song. A comedian always closed the bill – Jimmy Edwards, Tommy Trinder or Max Wall. When 'the cheeky chappie' Max Miller (pictured) came, my mother laughed so much that he pointed to her and called out: "Give that woman a free seat for tomorrow night."

Joan Bebbington, Crewe, Cheshire

Home hints

Make the most of all those TV ads with this reader's tip. 'During every TV ad break I get up and use the time to do a job. I tidy up, do the dishes, dust, clean a window – absolutely anything that needs doing. I even exercise! It's a great way to get things done while enjoying your favourite programme'

Mrs Bowen, Huddersfield

Wise words

"If in doubt do nowt"

I've always tried to live by this wisdom, to think things over and avoid rushing into anything. I find that, given time, things usually become clearer and you know what needs to be done.

Patricia Mason, Skipton

Headgear of yesteryear

This was my sister Doreen's wedding in June 1957. Me and my other sister, Eileen, are on the left, with Doreen's sisters-in-law on the right. The dresses and hats were Champagne coloured and we carried pink roses. Bridesmaids didn't always wear hats then, but Doreen had heard of the idea and loved it. The photographer arrived on his bicycle, camera in tow! He stayed around and took wonderful pictures all day. **Enid Fergie, Surbiton, Surrey**

On this week...

June 21, 1968 – Egg board gets pasting

There were calls for the Egg Marketing Board to be scrapped after claims that it was stifling competition in the egg market. The board was set up in 1957 to buy all eggs produced in the UK, grade them, stamp a 'Little Lion' on them, then market them through registered packhouses. The board was probably best known for its famous advertising slogan, 'Go to work on an egg' and finally closed in 1971.

Recipe of the week

Elderflower and Lime Cheesecake

Serves: 8
Preparation time:
Chilling time: 2–3 hours minimum

225g (8oz) digestive biscuits
100g (3 ½oz) unsalted butter
50g (2oz) sugar
400g (14oz) cream cheese
150ml (5 ¼fl.oz) double cream
Icing sugar, to taste
1 lime
Zest of 1 lemon
2 tbsp elderflower cordial
To decorate
Reserved crumbs and lime zest

1 Place the digestive biscuits in a large plastic bag. Hold one end of the bag and using a rolling pin, crush until they resemble fine breadcrumbs. Reserve a couple of spoonfuls of biscuit crumbs to decorate.
2 Melt the butter in a large saucepan, and add the crushed biscuits and sugar until fully combined.
3 Press the biscuit mixture firmly into a 20cm (8in) round tin with a lift up base and place in the fridge to set.
4 Meanwhile, wash the lemon and grate the skin using a fine grater or zester.
5 Place this zest together with the cream cheese, icing sugar and lime juice in a food processor and mix well.
6 Slowly add the cream and elderflower cordial until it is a smooth thick paste.
7 Spread the mixture over the biscuit base and chill for 2–3 hours, or overnight if preferred.
8 To release the cheesecake from the loose–bottomed tin, place on top of a glass and firmly press down on the sides of the tin which will slide down the cheesecake. Slip off the base onto the plate. Decorate with the reserved crumbs and lime zest.
© Belvoir Fruit Farms, www.belvoirfruitfarms.co.uk

23 Monday

24 Tuesday

25 Wednesday

26 Thursday

27 Friday

28 Saturday

29 Sunday

Every picture tells a story

Happy days with dad

This photo is of my sister, Patricia, my dad and myself in auntie's garden. I am on the left, aged about nine or ten. (Note the ribbons in our plaited hair – the most common hairstyle for girls then.)

I treasure this because I don't have any photos of my dad with us as children so it's extra special. There was no garden furniture as such, just a chair from the house. We were an ordinary working-class family – my dad worked for the Electricity Board and we lived in a council house – but my auntie was a bit posh so we would have been dressed in our Sunday best and on our best behaviour! She later emigrated to Australia.

Patricia and I both passed the 11-plus and went to Wolverhampton Girls' High School and I often wonder now how my mum, who worked for an engineering company, managed to find the money to pay for our expensive uniforms which had to be bought from Beatties department store.

Pauline Littler, Llanelli, Carmarthenshire

On this week...

June 27, 1963 – JFK charms Ireland
US President John F Kennedy received a rapturous welcome in County Wexford, Ireland, home of his great-grandfather Patrick Kennedy. One US photographer wept as the President joined a choir of 300 boys to sing the traditional song The Boys of Wexford. The President later visited his ancestral home in Dunganstown to be greeted with a kiss on the cheek by its current owner, Mary Ryan.

Home hints

Remove chewing gum from material by rubbing ice on it. Once it's frozen you can scrape it off. If this doesn't work you could also try heating it with a hairdryer and peeling it off. Then simply wash as normal. Make sure you wear gloves though as it's sticky stuff.

Wise words

"Your greatest gift is your freedom"
My grandfather was in France during the First World War and used to tell us stories of his time in the trenches. He taught us to value the freedom he and his comrades fought so hard to defend.

Sandra Cooper, Belvedere

Headgear of yesteryear

This is my mother wearing her best summer straw hat in 1932, when she would have been 37 years old. She always wore a hat – in the winter she wore felt hats that were a very similar shape to this but with a smaller brim. I loved dressing up and trying on her hats and, even though I was only 10 at the time, I always had my own hats to wear too.

Margaret Brooker, Lydbrook, Gloucestershire

Recipe of the week

Smoked salmon, Horseradish and Watercress Pasta

Serves: 4
Preparation time: 5 minutes
Cooking time: 10 minutes

300g (10 ½oz) penne pasta
Finely grated zest and juice of 1 lemon
1 tbsp cream horseradish sauce
150g (5 ¼oz) low-fat Greek style yoghurt
Salt and freshly ground black pepper
100g (3 ½oz) watercress, roughly chopped
100g (3 ½oz) smoked salmon, finely chopped

1 Cook the pasta in a large pan of boiling, salted water until it is just tender – about 10 minutes. Drain the pasta in a colander and return it to the pan.
2 Add the lemon zest and juice, horseradish, yoghurt and plenty of ground black pepper, then stir to coat the pasta. Add the salmon and watercress and stir gently to mix. Divide between four plates with more watercress on the side if liked.
© Watercress, www.watercress.co.uk

30	Monday

1	Tuesday

2	Wednesday

3	Thursday

4	Friday

5	Saturday

6	Sunday

Every picture tells a story

Fairies and firelight

My nanna had two sisters, Dolly and Lizzie. In 1952, my sister Judith and I spent a week of our school holidays with Great Auntie Lizzie and her husband, Wilf. They ran a small Post Office in the village of Draycott in Staffordshire.

They had no family of their own but they loved children. Great Uncle Wilf always swung us up in the air as soon as we arrived for a visit. As there was no electricity in their small cottage, light was provided by paraffin lamps which cast a lovely warm glow. There was no bathroom so we bathed in a tin bath in front of the fire.

Our days were spent helping Great Uncle Wilf in the workshop where he did his carpentry or playing in the fields. We found a large 'fairy ring' (a large circle of grass surrounded by low raised banks) and were convinced that the fairies came out and danced there in the evening, although we never saw them. We were disappointed to learn that in fact it had once been a cockpit before cock fighting was banned.

Angela J Wilson, Ruislip, Middx

On this week...

July 5, 1975 – Ashe makes Wimbledon history
American tennis player Arthur Ashe became the first black man to win the Wimbledon men's singles, after beating fellow American Jimmy Connors three sets to one. The crowd turned against Connors when he lost his cool during the match, swearing and angrily throwing his towel under the umpire's chair. But afterwards he graciously said of Ashe: "Everything he did was good."

Home hints

Give your lawn some TLC – particularly if you forgot to feed it in spring or if it's looking a bit bare. If the weather isn't too hot, you may need to cut it every week, but don't go too short as this can leave grass weak and unable to compete with weeds and moss. Apply a lawn feed regularly too, and treat moss or weed patches.

Wise words

"To the world you may be one person, but to one person you may be the world."
My wonderful dad had so many little sayings and phrases that he quoted all the time it's hard to pick a favourite, but this one does give me a warm feeling.
Eve Fletcher, Skelmersdale

Headgear of yesteryear

This photo was taken in 1948 when I was 20 years old and working in a department store called Potts and Sons. My green and white dress was a Kitty Copland label, but I made the hat myself with garden raffia plaited and sewn into shape – we were ingenious in those days! I later agreed to write to a young man and sent him this photo – we have just celebrated our Diamond Wedding.
Joan Cuthbertson, Erith, Kent

Recipe of the week

Strawberry and Coconut Ice Lollies

Makes: 8
Preparation time: 20 minutes, plus 4 hours freezing

400g (14oz) strawberries, washed and hulled
3 tbsp icing sugar
400g (14oz) coconut Greek yoghurt
You will also need
Lolly moulds and sticks

1 Using a blender or food processor, purée 200g (7oz) of the strawberries with the icing sugar. Remove and sieve to separate and discard the seeds.
2 In a large jug, mix the strawberry purée with the coconut yoghurt and fill the lolly moulds (but not quite to the top).
3 Slice the remaining strawberries and divide these between the mould, pushing them down carefully so they are evenly distributed throughout the lolly.
4 Push in the lolly sticks and freeze for at least four hours, or until completely set.

Top tip: Warm the moulds with your hands or under warm water to release the lollies.
© Driscoll Jubilee Strawberries, www.jubileestrawberries.co.uk

7 Monday

8 Tuesday

9 Wednesday

10 Thursday

11 Friday

12 Saturday

13 Sunday

Every picture tells a story

A whirlwind romance

In 1966, my friend and I went on holiday to Italy. Four young men from Manchester arrived to stay at our hotel. My friend fancied the tallish slim one while I liked the look of the stocky one with curly hair. He never looked at me once!

Instead, I spent time with the tall one who wore dark glasses and hardly said a word, but he was really kind and thoughtful. The romance didn't end with the holiday, as I thought it would, but living 300 miles apart made courtship difficult so the decision was made to get married soon.

The wedding was lovely, but the first year we were married was very hard. I had married someone I hardly knew and I was homesick for Scotland and my family. It was only made easier by the kindness of my mother-in-law and my young husband, Colin, who never faltered and never once thought we had made a mistake.

More than 40 years on, we have two sons and six grandsons and I have no regrets about marrying a 'stranger'.

Janice Jackson, Preston, Lancs

On this week...

July 13, 1985 – Live Aid is a smash hit
The Live Aid concert for people starving in Africa raised three times the £10 million hoped for by the organisers. A crowd of 72,000 joined Prince Charles and Princess Diana in Wembley Stadium, and a host of stars flew in from around the globe. Television viewers responded in their thousands when Bob Geldof implored: "Don't go to the pub tonight – please stay in and give us your money."

Home hints

Harvest your runner beans when the pods reach 15-20cm (6-8in) in length and pick regularly to encourage more to come. Runner beans are a great source of vitamin K, which is important for maintaining healthy bones. Steam them to help ensure the nutritional value remains intact.

Wise words

"If you have a problem, there is a solution"
My father frequently quoted these wise words, followed closely by: "If there's no solution then you don't have a problem – you have a fact that you will have to learn to live with." I know I didn't appreciate him as much as I should but dad's words have remained with me.

Kathy Regan, Carmarthen

Headgear of yesteryear

This is a photo of me and my friend Suzette Ashton at a wedding in 1964 – the perfect occasion for a hat! I am wearing the cream coat with navy and cream hat, navy shoes, bag and gloves. Suzette is in the pink with a navy hat and gloves. I lost touch with Suzette a long time ago but would love to hear from her if she sees this picture.

Joyce Hardy, Southampton, Hampshire

Recipe of the week

Leek, Mackerel and Avocado Salad
Serves: 2
Preparation time: 15 minutes

1 leek, roughly chopped
4 handfuls rocket
1 avocado, diced
2 fillets smoked mackerel, diced
8 cherry tomatoes, halved
Juice of $^1/_2$ lemon
Handful of fresh dill, torn
4 tsp toasted mixed seeds
Dash of virgin olive oil
Freshly ground black pepper

1 Steam the leek for about 2 minutes, until tender.
2 Put the rocket, leek, avocado, smoked mackerel and tomatoes into a large serving bowl. Squeeze over the lemon juice.
3 Add the dill, seeds, olive oil and black pepper and toss lightly together.
© British Leeks, www.british-leeks.co.uk

14 Monday

15 Tuesday

16 Wednesday

17 Thursday

18 Friday

19 Saturday

20 Sunday

Every picture tells a story

Railway ways

I love this photo of my late father taken on our annual summer holiday in the Fifties – it is so reminiscent of the period as he is dressed in a suit, shirt and tie for a day on the beach.

I remember that my mother would wear a suit for the train journey while my brother and I travelled in our school blazers and my brother also wore his school cap. My parents saved for our seaside break by paying into a holiday club at work. We usually went for two weeks in August, staying in a guesthouse, although once we had a chalet in someone's garden in Westward Ho!

The day of our departure was always very exciting. We got up when it was still dark and walked to the bus stop where we caught the first bus to Wolverhampton station and boarded a steam train. We didn't have too much luggage to carry as a trunk had already been sent ahead by rail and would be waiting for us on arrival at our accommodation. Those were the days!

Margaret Jesson, Bridgnorth, Shropshire

On this week...

July 17, 2000 – Tesco reverts to imperial
Supermarket chain Tesco decided to put imperial measures back on packets, as well as metric, after confusion among customers. A survey had revealed that nine out of ten customers still thought in imperial when buying food. One customer ordered 3kg (6.6lb) of broccoli while ordering online instead of 3lb, while another ordered 9kg (19.8lb) of potatoes instead of 9lb.

Home hints

Scrub your nails with an old toothbrush and lemon juice. This natural bleaching agent will help get rid of any old nail polish staining and will help whiten them too. To get the most from your nail polish, avoid shaking, as this will cause air bubbles. Instead roll it in your palms to loosen and mix the colour.

Wise words

"Accept people for what they are and not what you'd like them to be"

When going through a dark time in my life I learned that we are all human and handle situations differently. It's not an easy lesson to live by but well worth remembering.

Rita Stephens, South Elmsall

Headgear of yesteryear

I loved this floppy hat, pictured in 1972, as it matched the outfit bought by my boyfriend on a ski trip to Austria. I wore it to many weddings at the time. We will celebrate 41 happy years of marriage this July, and during those years the hat has been suitably decorated for our various amateur dramatic participations, including the role of Eliza Doolittle in My Fair Lady!

Serena Blair, Coleraine, Northern Ireland

Recipe of the week

Pear and Almond Puffs

Makes: 8
Preparation time: 20 minutes
Cooking time: 15 minutes

500g (1lb 1 $^{1}/_{2}$oz) all butter puff pastry block, thawed
4 ripe pears (choose the rounded variety rather than longer ones)
100g (3 $^{1}/_{2}$oz) marzipan
3 tbsp jam, for glazing
Beaten egg white
Caster sugar, for sprinkling

1 Preheat oven to 220°C/425°F/Gas Mark 7.
2 Peel all the pears, halve and remove core. Fill cavities with marzipan.
3 Roll out pastry to a rectangle approx. 20x40cm (8x16in) and cut into 8 equal squares.
4 With a sharp knife, slice through the pears but leave stem end intact. Place one pear half diagonally on a pastry square, pressing pear lightly to slightly 'fan' it. Brush the pastry edges with beaten egg white then bring up the corner nearest the rounded end of the pear and press onto pear. Brush again and sprinkle with caster sugar.
5 Bake for 12-15 minutes until pastry is risen and golden.
6 Gently heat jam and sieve to remove the large pieces of fruit. Brush each pear with melted jam and allow to cool before serving.

© Jus-Rol, www.jusrol.co.uk

21 Monday

22 Tuesday

23 Wednesday

24 Thursday

25 Friday

26 Saturday

27 Sunday

Every picture tells a story

The joy of candy floss

With the beaches encased in barbed wire, seaside holidays weren't possible in wartime. Instead, Slough Council came up with a brilliant alternative – two weeks of local attractions ranging from a fun fair to fireworks and a competition for a carnival queen.

To stage many of these events the council took over a huge field called Agar's Plough that belonged to Eton College. As a little girl of seven, I was delighted and the photo shows me with my mother about to set off to the opening ceremony. I was rather scared of the fairground rides, but enjoyed watching them. We rushed over to see the Bonny Baby competition.

In those days, a bonny baby was a fat baby – and some of them were really fat! Next, we came across a candy floss stall. I had never seen candy floss before and part of the excitement was watching it being spun and growing into a great big pink ball. And oh, the taste! To me, it was like something from fairyland.

Muriel Aird, Weymouth, Dorset

Home hints

Use olive oil as a skin and nail booster. Massage it onto your skin then wipe away with cotton wool to remove make-up or for a skin-softening treat simply massage in and lay a warm damp flannel over your face. To moisturise nails and soften cuticles add a few drops to a bowl of warm water and soak your nails for 5-10 minutes.

Wise words

"WE comes before I in wedding"
On the day that my husband George and I were married a friend gave us this advice. We must have taken it on board because we've been married now for 52 years.   **Maureen Thayre, Dundee**

Headgear of yesteryear

This is my favourite hat picture. Our two granddaughters, Jessica and Philippa, were staying with us for the weekend, and we took them to Rufford Abbey in Nottingham on this lovely sunny day. Philippa, who was nearly three years old, kept the sun off her by borrowing Granddad's straw hat! Both the girls are now grown up and live away from home, but we are all still close, and photos like these bring back great memories.
                Cynthia Lyon, Grantham, Lincolnshire

On this week...

July 24, 1987 – Record payment for Archer
Former deputy chair of the Conservative Party, Jeffrey Archer, was awarded record libel damages at the High Court. The Daily Star newspaper was ordered to pay him £500,000 damages, plus up to £700,000 costs. The paper had printed a front-page story alleging Mr Archer had paid to have sex with a prostitute. Before leaving the court he shook each of the jurors by the hand saying: "The verdict speaks for itself."

Recipe of the week

Spanish Omelette

Serves: 2
Preparation time: 15–25 minutes
Cooking time: 15 minutes

1 medium onion, thinly sliced
6 large eggs
2 tbsp olive oil
Salt and pepper
4 medium potatoes (pre–cooked or leftovers), diced
Large handful frozen peas

1 Heat the oil until fairly hot. Warm the potatoes through and add the onions for five minutes, until cooked but not brown. Drain the potato mixture and keep the oil (allow them to cool!).
2 Beat the eggs with salt and pepper, add the potato mixture and stir well. It works well set aside for 10 minutes at this point but it's not essential.
3 Heat a little of the oil saved earlier in a medium frying pan. Add the mixture and peas, and cook until brown on the bottom. Turn using a couple of plates (this will be a bit messy) then brown the other side. Add more oil if the pan is dry.
4 The omelette is cooked when brown on both sides and a little runny in the middle – this should take approximately 10 minutes. Brush with a little of the reserved olive oil. Can be served warm, or cold the next day.

Top tip: Cooking potatoes from raw? Traditionally you should add them first to the hot oil, and cook gently without browning them, for 12-15 minutes. Then add the onions and continue as directed.
© Potato Council, www.manyfacesofpotatoes.co.uk

28 Monday

29 Tuesday

30 Wednesday

31 Thursday

1 Friday

2 Saturday

3 Sunday

Every picture tells a story

A magical island

I was 12 when I had my first holiday. In 1966 I went with my mother and brother to the Isle of Man. We flew there which made it seem like a real adventure.

When we got off the plane at Ronaldsway airport, I thought I'd landed in another world, it was so different from our home near Sheffield. From the coach that took us to our hotel in Douglas, I saw blue tiled roofs and magnificent palm trees swaying in the breeze. Our hotel was on the promenade, overlooking the sea. There was no shortage of things to do.

I loved riding on the horse-drawn trams that ran along the front and also going on 'mystery tour' coach trips that took you to Rushen Abbey where we would have strawberries and cream while a band played. We sometimes took a relaxing walk in Summerhill Glen and while ambling about might come across a Manx cat with no tail. I simply fell in love with the place and have had a soft spot for it ever since. **Linda Spooner, Sheffield**

On this week...

July 30, 1991 – Pavarotti sings in the rain
A rain-soaked crowd of 100,000 people watched legendary Italian tenor Luciano Pavarotti perform in London's Hyde Park. The concert was to celebrate 30 years in opera and was the biggest musical event the park had seen since the Rolling Stones performed there in 1969. By the end of the night, the St John Ambulance had treated 193 people for the effects of the cold.

Home hints

Prolong your flowering plants by deadheading regularly and remember to keep on top of watering plants. If you're going on holiday move patio plants into a shaded area, water well and cover with shade netting material available from garden centres. Keep indoor plants healthy by soaking a towel, laying it in the bath and standing your plants on it.

Wise words

"Use what talents you possess; the woods would be silent if no birds sang but those who sang the best"
My father often repeated this quote from Henry Van Dyke (American author and clergyman). He encouraged my five siblings and me to be true to our abilities and I've encouraged my children in the same way.

Dorothy Hickson, Milford Haven

Headgear of yesteryear

This is a photo of my mother, Edith, on the left. It was taken more than 50 years ago in 1962, and shows her at a family wedding with her three sisters – Rose, Frances and Jane. Don't they all look smart? The hats, gloves and handbags are all so similar that I think they must have been very in fashion at the time. My cousins Jean and Harold, who were married on this day, recently celebrated their Golden Wedding.
Susan Pearce, Wolverhampton, West Midlands

Recipe of the week

Pearl Barley Paella

Serves: 6
Preparation time: 20 minutes
Cooking time: 1 ½ hours, plus 20 minutes

225g (8oz) pearl barley
2 chicken or vegetable stock cubes
50g (2oz) butter
Pinch saffron
1 large Spanish onion, finely chopped
1 red pepper, deseeded and chopped
110g (4oz) cooking chorizo, sliced
110g (4oz) bacon lardons or thick bacon, diced
2 cloves garlic, finely chopped
1 tsp soft thyme leaves, plus extra to garnish
1 tsp smoked paprika
1/4 tsp dried red chilli flakes
120ml (4fl.oz) dry white wine
400g (14oz) can chopped tomatoes
110g (4oz) fresh or frozen peas
225g (8oz) cooked peeled prawns
To serve
Sprigs of thyme

1 Put the pearl barley into a large saucepan and add enough water to cover generously. Add the stock cubes, bring to the boil, then reduce the heat and simmer for 1 ½ hours until tender, topping up the water if necessary.
2 Melt the butter in a large frying pan or wok and gently sauté the saffron, onion and pepper for 5 minutes. Add the chorizo and bacon and fry on a higher heat for a further 5 minutes.
3 Add the garlic, thyme, paprika, chilli, wine, tomatoes and peas to this pan. Bring to the boil, then simmer for 5 more minutes. Stir in the prawns and simmer for 2 minutes to heat them through.
6 Drain the pearl barley thoroughly and stir through the other ingredients, making sure it is piping hot. Serve, garnished with a few thyme sprigs.
© Romana Richards for Kerrygold, www.kerrygold.co.uk

4 Monday

5 Tuesday

6 Wednesday

7 Thursday

8 Friday

9 Saturday

10 Sunday

Every picture tells a story

A guide for life

During the week Mollie Brice was a Latin teacher and on Fridays she ran the Teignmouth Grammar School company of Girl Guides. She was an encouraging and inspirational role model who opened our eyes to the locality and the wider community. In the Fifties I enjoyed going to Girl Guide meetings with more than 30 other girls.

Mollie prepared us for summer camps which were held at Seaton, Bude, Cornwood and Widecombe-in-the-Moor. Dartmoor was best for hiking, exploring, looking for birds, flowers and wildlife. When it rained, we slept in barns, old cowsheds or stables. Whatever the weather, Mollie's warm smile and hard work made everyone feel good.

She embodied all the virtues of being trusty, loyal, helpful and friendly that were instilled into us as Guides. Mollie made a positive difference to my life and those of countless others. She wrote to me for over 30 years.

Marian Rich, Andover, Hants

On this week...

August 9, 1979 – Nudists welcomed to Brighton
The seaside town of Brighton announced that it planned to become the first resort in Britain to open one of its beaches to nudists. The town's leaders hoped the move would increase tourism but many residents were up in arms about the move. "People naively believe what is good for the continent is good for Britain," said councillor John Blackman.

Home hints

Harvest your black and redcurrants and blackberries this week and make them into jams and chutneys. To see if your jam has set, pop a couple of saucers in the freezer. Put a spoonful of jam onto a saucer and leave for a minute. If it wrinkles and has a sort of skin when you touch it then it's set.

Wise words

"The secret of good whites is in the rinsing"
When I was due to get married in 1968 mum gave me this advice. Two years later I had two babies and a stack of terry nappies, which were always rinsed under the outside tap until every trace of soap powder was gone. I'm still proud of my whites thanks to mum.

Anne Stones, Grimsby

Headgear of yesteryear

This is a picture of me at my son's wedding. I chose a very pale green Jaeger coat but couldn't find a matching hat. I bought a beige fine straw hat but knew it wouldn't look good with the pale green. One day I was with my husband in B&Q, wandered off down the paint aisle and saw a tiny can of delicate green car touch-up paint. I bought it, and sprayed my new beige hat. It was a wonderful match!

Josie Birkett, Camberley, Surrey

Recipe of the week

Apple and Spinach Salad

Serves: 2
Preparation time: 10 minutes
Cooking time: 5 minutes

50g (2oz) slivered almonds or hazelnuts
2 tbsp sugar
170g (6oz) baby spinach leaves
1 head romaine lettuce, washed and torn
2 Cameo apples, cored and thinly sliced
For the dressing
$1/4$ red onion, finely chopped
6 tbsp apple cider vinegar
6 tbsp olive oil
3 tbsp sugar
1 clove garlic, minced (optional)
$1/4$ tsp salt
Pinch freshly ground black pepper
To serve
Handful sugared almonds

1 Place almonds or hazelnuts in a medium pan with the sugar. Stir constantly over a medium–high heat for 4 minutes, or until coated and browned. Set aside.
2 Combine the dressing ingredients in a small bowl and stir through. Pour over spinach, lettuce and apples just before serving.
3 Toss, and sprinkle with sugared almonds.
© Cameo Apples, www.cameoapple.co.uk

11 Monday

12 Tuesday

13 Wednesday

14 Thursday

15 Friday

16 Saturday

17 Sunday

Every picture tells a story

Ever the best of pals

This is my husband John (in front) with his great friend, Ben. They are rehearsing their special act, Strolling by Bud Flanagan and Chesney Allen, which they performed in many local venues including New Road Side working men's club in Wyke. There was never a dull moment when they were around – they were always laughing.

John was a welder and Ben was a fitter; both men worked at Low Moor steel works near Bradford until it closed down in 1983. Our two families were always very close and John was godfather to Ben's son, also named John. Ben didn't drive, so when he stood for election to Bradford City Council, John acted as his chauffeur. (Ben eventually held the office of Deputy Lord Mayor in the 1960s.)

Sadly, John and Ben are no longer with us but Ben's widow, Betty, and I keep in touch. We often wonder if our husbands are still together as they were in life, entertaining the angels with their double act!

Margaret Dean, Bradford, W Yorkshire

On this week...

August 11, 2010 – Cat sets purring record
Farm cat Smokey set the world record for loudest purring at his home near Northampton. Smokey's record-breaking 67.7-decibel purr was recorded in the presence of a vet, a representative of Northampton Cats Protection, a local MP and a sound engineer. His owner, Lucinda, gave him plenty of encouragement with a grooming brush, lots of stroking and slices of ham.

Home hints

Drink enough water. We all know that we should be drinking two litres (8-10 glasses) of water a day, but thirst is often mistaken for hunger. In between meals, when you feel hungry, first have a glass of water and see if it helps. Water is important for flushing out toxins and keeping wrinkles at bay.

Wise words

"Don't look down on anyone, unless you're helping them up"
When I was younger mum told me this, at a time when many people were down on their luck. She instilled in me that I was no better or worse than anyone else – but just as good as.

Gloria Wilding, Prescot

Headgear of yesteryear

This photo shows me wearing the sunhat I made in 1940 from strips of cellophane, which was leftover from the packaging at the grocery store where I worked. Once I had made the hat, I managed to scrape together the money to have this professional photograph taken. I was delighted when I went to collect my photo and found it was on display in the shop window in full colour!

Phyllis Wright, Basingstoke, Hampshire

Recipe of the week

Greek Olive and Yoghurt Bread

Makes: 2 loaves
Preparation time: 25 minutes, plus 30-40 minutes proving
Cooking time: 25-30 minutes

500g (1lb 1 $^1/_2$oz) Wright's ciabatta bread mix
200g (7oz) natural Greek yoghurt
175ml (fl.oz) warm water
2 tbsp olive oil
100g (3 $^1/_2$oz) pitted black olives
75g (3oz) ground rice, for dusting

1 Place the bread mix into a mixing bowl. Add the yoghurt, warm water and olive oil then mix together to form a soft dough. Knead for 5 minutes, dusting with a little ground rice if necessary.
2 Cover loosely with a damp tea towel, lightly oiled plastic or polythene and allow to rest for 5 minutes. Meanwhile, coarsely chop the olives in half.
3 Again, using ground rice to dust, mix the olives evenly through the dough, then divide into two equal pieces. Shape each piece into a ball then elongate to a torpedo shape.
4 Place the loaves onto a large, pre-lined baking tray that has been liberally sprinkled with ground rice and dust top of the loaves with ground rice too. Loosely cover again and leave to rise in a warm place for 30-40 minutes, or until the dough has doubled in size.
5 Gently cut a pattern on top of each loaf with a sharp knife. Bake in a preheated oven at 225°C/437°F/Gas Mark 7 for 25-30 minutes until well-risen and deep golden brown.

Top Tip: The loaf should sound hollow when tapped on the base.

© Wright's Home Baking, www.wrightsflour.co.uk

18 Monday

19 Tuesday

20 Wednesday

21 Thursday

22 Friday

23 Saturday

24 Sunday

Every picture tells a story

The Open University

A degree of success

When I was 64 my daughter completed a degree course with the Open University and suggested I should do the same. I sent off for details and was amazed that having only four 'O' levels didn't matter.

I was thrilled to pass my exam at the end of the first year, but suffered a setback in my second year when I had to care for my elderly aunt and uncle. To my relief, I passed, but when I only just scraped through at the end of my third year, I became dejected.

Then I discovered I was suffering from diabetes which was one reason for my depression. I had treatment and embarked on my fourth year of studies. Despite the death of my aunt during that time, I managed to pass with a respectable mark.

For my final year, I chose a course on creative writing and began to have faith in my ability to achieve my aim. Imagine my pride when I received my degree at the age of 70!

Anne Yeates, Newent, Glos

On this week...

August 24, 1967 – Penguins cool off in heatwave
Two penguins from Chessington Zoo enjoyed a day trip to an ice-rink to cool off during a heat wave. As temperatures headed for 80°F (27°C), Rocky the Rockhopper penguin and his female companion joined skaters at the Silver Blades ice-rink in London's Streatham. Staff were so impressed with the penguins' performance on the ice that they extended the invitation to the zoo's other 20 penguins!

Home hints

Prevent pongy pussy cats. Cat litter trays can be a smelly affair. Clean them regularly and try mixing in a little baking soda with your usual litter to help absorb bad smells.

Wise words

"Relax!"

This one word is the best piece of advice I've ever been given. It helped me through all life's stresses from childhood exams to childbirth and, more recently, caring for my parents. My father had it printed on a sign for me as a permanent reminder so I can never forget it – or him!

Mary Ashley, Weston-Super-Mare

Headgear of yesteryear

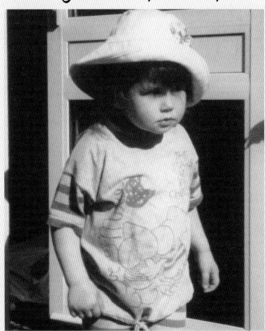

This photograph is of my granddaughter Olivia when she was three years old, on her weekly visit to our house with her mother and younger brother, Kieran. We were sitting out in the garden, but Olivia really didn't want to wear this hat to protect her from the sun. In fact, just after the photo was taken she threw it straight off! She is now 20 and still as determined about things as she was then!

Marjorie Duncan, Kirkcaldy, Fife

Recipe of the week

Caramel Poached Blueberries with Crème Fraîche

Serves: 4
Preparation time: 10 minutes
Cooking time: 10 minutes

150g (5 ¼oz) caster sugar
3 tbsp cold water
2 tbsp boiling water
150g (5 ¼oz) blueberries
To serve
250ml (9fl.oz) crème fraîche
250g (9oz) natural Greek yoghurt

1 Add the sugar and cold water to a medium frying pan and heat very gently, stirring only occasionally until the sugar has completely dissolved – this should take about 5 minutes. Increase the heat and boil for 3-4 minutes without stirring, until the syrup thickens and then begins to turn golden around the edges. Watch very closely as the syrup begins to colour and tilt the pan gently from time to time to even this colour out. Cook for a minute or two more until golden all over.
2 Take the pan off the heat and add the boiling water, remembering to stand well back as the syrup will spit. As soon as the bubbles begin to subside, tilt the pan to mix the syrup with the extra water.
3 Add the blueberries and cook for 1 minute or until the juices just begin to run from the blueberries, then leave to cool.
4 Stir the crème fraîche and Greek yoghurt together in a bowl and chill until needed.
5 When ready to serve, add alternate spoonfuls of the yoghurt mixture and the caramelised blueberries to 4 serving glasses. Serve like this, or, for a marbled effect, run a small knife or teaspoon handle through each to swirl together.
© Seasonal Berries, www.seasonalberries.co.uk

25 Monday

26 Tuesday

27 Wednesday

28 Thursday

29 Friday

30 Saturday

31 Sunday

Every picture tells a story

Worth waiting for!

Although I met my future wife, Wynne, in 1937 when she was 15 and I was 16, we didn't marry until 1944. We became friends while we were both on holiday in Great Yarmouth.

After she returned home to Yorkshire and I was back in Birmingham we wrote to each other. When war broke out, I joined the Army and Wynne was a nurse in London so we didn't meet very often. In October 1943, we were both on leave, staying with my parents, when I proposed.

We planned to marry in June 1944 but in March my regiment was moved down to the south coast in preparation for D-Day. My commanding officer said: "Weren't you were planning to get married? You'd better buzz off quickly while you can get leave." So our wedding was brought forward to May. In 2014 we'll celebrate our 70th anniversary and I still love her to bits.

Den Rollason, Sutton Coldfield, W Midlands

On this week...

August 25, 1974 – Human cannonball misses target

Mary Connors, 21, tried to sail over the River Avon and land in a safety net after being fired from a giant cannon. This was her second attempt to be shot further than anyone else in England and break the existing record. Unfortunately, Mary, a secretary, fell short and ended up in the water. Luckily, she later told reporters, she had taken 'a few swimming lessons'.

Home hints

Dry skin can leave your lipstick looking patchy, uneven and can really add on the years. Banish dry skin by gently exfoliating lips regularly – an old toothbrush is perfect for this or make your own scrub by mixing everyday granulated sugar with almond or olive oil.

Wise words

"Never want more than you've got"
My nan, who lived to be nearly 91, used this as her mantra throughout her life. I find it a refreshing antidote to a modern materialistic society.
Mary Cook, Market Rasen

Headgear of yesteryear

I love this photo of my mum on her summer holidays in Blackpool in the late Fifties. She and my grandparents always went there during Barnsley Feast Week, when everyone would crowd to the beaches. Blackpool has remained a favourite family destination, and I too have wonderful childhood memories there, so it's great to see my mum having such a good time. Of course, Blackpool has changed a lot since then!
Moira Brooks, Barnsley, South Yorkshire

Recipe of the week

Potato and Chickpea Curry
Serves: 4
Preparation time: 10 minutes
Cooking time: 20 minutes

1 tbsp oil
1 onion, sliced
2 cloves garlic, crushed
4 medium potatoes, King Edward or Maris Piper, cubed with skin on
2 tbsp medium madras curry paste
2 tbsp tomato purée
240g (8 ¹/₂oz) chick peas, drained
2 tbsp mango chutney
300ml (¹/₂ pt) vegetable stock
¹/₄ cucumber, finely chopped
2 tbsp fresh coriander, chopped

1 Heat 1 tbsp of olive oil in a large saucepan, add the onion and garlic and sweat for 1-2 minutes.
2 Add the potatoes, curry paste, purée, chick peas and chutney. Combine well and heat through for 1-2 minutes.
3 Add the stock and bring to the boil, cover with lid and fast simmer for about 15-20 minutes until the potatoes are soft.
4 Serve sprinkled with cucumber and coriander.
Top Tip: For an even quicker option, add a 500g (1lb 1 ¹/₂oz) jar curry sauce instead of the stock and curry paste.
© Potato Council, www.manyfacesofpotatoes.co.uk

1 Monday

2 Tuesday

3 Wednesday

4 Thursday

5 Friday

6 Saturday

7 Sunday

Every picture tells a story

PIC: REX FEATURES

Doris was our darling

My sister Sheila and I loved Doris Day. We used to go and see all her films. Worthing had two cinemas in those days and we would queue up on a Saturday evening to see a film and, if we didn't have anything to do on Sunday, we would go back and watch it all over again!

When we went to see Doris in Calamity Jane, we laughed so much that the manager told us to be quiet as we were disturbing other people. We had our hair styled like Doris's and dressed like her, but we couldn't sing like her (although we tried). My poor dad used to get mad with us, saying we shouldn't copy film stars, filling our heads with silly ideas – but it didn't stop us.

He was quite strict and even when Sheila was 21, he didn't approve of her wearing make-up. She was told: "Go back upstairs and take that muck off your face!"

Janet Dudman, Worthing

On this week...

September 1, 1985 – Wreck of Titanic located
The wreck of the HMS Titanic was located by a team of scientists led by oceanographer Dr Robert Ballard. The first object to be sighted by an unmanned submarine was one of the ship's huge boilers followed by the ship's hull, upright and lying 13,000ft below the surface. The team's cheers and clapping were quickly replaced by a reverential silence. It was 2am – very close to the time the great ship had sunk.

Home hints

Now's the time to dig up remaining potatoes before they get damaged by slugs. Autumn is one of the best seasons to plant as the ground remains warm and plants have a chance to get settled before the cold weather comes. Now's the time to plant evergreens through to October, or wait until March.

Wise words

"There's no such thing as a free lunch"
My boss used to say this to me and how right he was! Over the years I've found that few people give anything away freely without expecting something in return.   **Kath Easton, London**

Headgear of yesteryear

This is a photograph of myself when I was 16 years old, dated 5 September 1939 – two days after war was declared. I felt I was growing up and wanted to have the photo taken to mark this time in my life. My grandma bought me this lovely blue hat with gold chain wrapped around it. I wore it with a grey mixture Harris Tweed suit and chocolate brown suede court shoes.
                    Doris Bird, Gosport, Hampshire

Recipe of the week

Chilli with Crispy Paprika Croutons

Serves: 4
Preparation time: 15 minutes
Cooking time: 1 hour simmering, plus 10 minutes

2 tbsp vegetable oil
1 large onion, chopped
1 red pepper, chopped
500g (1lb 1 $^{1}/_{2}$oz) minced beef
1 tbsp flour
400g (14oz) chopped tomatoes
300ml ($^{1}/_{2}$pt) beef stock
1 tbsp tomato purée
1 tbsp mild chilli powder
1 tbsp dark brown sugar
400g (14oz) red kidney beans, drained
For the croutons
4 tbsp vegetable oil
$^{1}/_{2}$ tsp paprika
$^{1}/_{4}$ tsp chilli powder
2 garlic cloves, crushed
3 thick slices bread, cut into cubes
To serve
Fresh coriander, chopped and served with sour cream

1 Soften onion and red pepper in the oil, add minced beef and brown quickly.
2 Stir in the flour and then add tomatoes, stock, purée, chilli powder, sugar and kidney beans. Bring to the boil and then simmer gently for 1 hour. Season to taste.
3 For the croutons, heat the oil in a large frying pan and add the paprika, chilli powder and garlic. Add the bread cubes and toss until well coated. Place on a baking tray in a hot oven until golden. Serve chilli topped with croutons, chopped coriander and sour cream.
© Flour Advisory Bureau, www.fabflour.co.uk

8	Monday

9	Tuesday

10	Wednesday

11	Thursday

12	Friday

13	Saturday

14	Sunday

Every picture tells a story

Dog overboard!

This handsome hound was our family's much-loved Labrador, Danny, pictured on a boat on the Norfolk Broads. Danny joined in all our activities with great gusto and especially enjoyed our holidays afloat. Invariably, he fell overboard at least once during the week and had to be rescued by my brothers. One of them dived in after him while the other one rowed the dinghy over to ferry him back to the boat.

The rest of us stood on deck, shouting helpful instructions, while my mother waited with a towel to rub him down. From the first, he fitted in perfectly with our family's somewhat chaotic lifestyle and he was never what you'd call a well-trained dog.

My father used to joke that Danny never did what we told him because he knew he had a better pedigree than we did!

Marion Wilson, Cranfield, Beds

On this week...

September 13, 1980 – Hercules the missing bear found

A bear that had been taking part in the filming of a Kleenex commercial was found and captured after 24 days on the run. Hercules, who stood 8 ft 4 in (2.54 m) and weighed half a ton, was spotted swimming in water by a local crofter in the Outer Hebrides. Hercules' owner, wrestler Andy Robin, was overjoyed to be reunited with him and the two enjoyed regular TV appearances throughout the 1980s.

Home hints

Recycle old greetings cards. They can be made into gift tags, bookmarks and even into new cards. If you're not crafty then you can usually recycle them to worthy causes over the festive period or ask at your local school or nursery as they may take them to add to their craft supplies.

Wise words

"Neither a borrower or a lender be"
My father often used to say this and, although I've done both over the years, I can see how it could break up friendships or even families as well as cause financial difficulties.

Nancy French, Aberdeen

Headgear of yesteryear

This is a photograph of me in a hat worn at my daughter Janet's wedding in 1981. I didn't wear hats that often at the time, but I do think they complete an outfit, and the bride's mother has to have a hat! The day was very memorable, and the weather was great. When the happy couple left for their honeymoon, some joker had fixed a pair of kippers to the exhaust pipe of their car!

Beryl Kelsey, Upminster, Essex

Recipe of the week

Spicy Fish Cakes with Salad and Yoghurt Dip

Serves: 1
Preparation time: 45 minutes
Cooking time: 45 minutes

200g (7oz) sweet potato, cut into wedges
Salt and freshly ground pepper
Drizzle olive oil
Paprika spice mix
100g (3 1/2oz) salmon
50g (2oz) prawns
1/2 tsp red Thai curry paste
Pinch salt
25g (1oz) runner beans
160g (5 1/2oz) salad – lettuce, cucumber, spinach and celery mix
10g (1/4oz) coconut oil
For the dip
40g (1 1/2oz) Greek yoghurt
Handful fresh coriander leaves, chopped
1/4 chilli, finely chopped

1 Preheat the oven to 375°F/190°C/Gas Mark 5.
2 Place the wedges into a bowl, mix with salt and pepper and the spice mix (to taste) and place on a baking tray. Cook in the middle of an oven for 45 minutes.
3 Place the salmon, prawns, curry paste, coriander and salt into a food processor and blend until it has formed a paste. Add the runner beans and then blend at a higher speed. Transfer mixture to a bowl and chill for 10 minutes.
4 Prepare the salad on a serving plate.
5 Make sure your hands are cool, then shape the fish mixture into small patties.
6 Heat the oil in a frying pan and fry the patties for 10 minutes on each side, over low heat.
7 Prepare the dip by mixing coriander and chilli with the Greek yoghurt.
8 Once the wedges have nicely crisped and the fish cakes are ready, arrange on the serving plate along with the yoghurt dip.

© Total, www.totalgreekyoghurt.com

15 Monday

16 Tuesday

17 Wednesday

18 Thursday

19 Friday

20 Saturday

21 Sunday

Every picture tells a story

Setting a good example

My mum was an inspiration to me because she was a very down-to-earth woman who got on with things. Money was not very plentiful but we managed to have good food and clean clothes always. We lived in Colliery Cottages as dad worked for the Coal Board.

He had a weak chest and suffered from bronchitis every winter. When I was eight he had to go into hospital with pleurisy and pneumonia. We used to go on the bus to see him every day. Luckily, he recovered. Mum was a great cook; she made lovely pies and puddings and won a set of scales for her pastry.

I always had a party for my birthday – mum made the cake and dad iced it. They were great parents who taught me the value of things and always to be kind to people. Their motto was 'do as you would be done by'.

Ann Rowlatt, Deeping St James, Lincs

On this week...

September 21, 1955 – Britain claims Rockall
A small party led by naval officer Lieutenant Commander Desmond Scott raised a Union flag and cemented a plaque onto the tiny island of Rockall, 300 miles west of Scotland. The rocky 21m (70ft) high islet was annexed to stop the Soviets using it as a watchtower to spy on British missile tests in the Hebrides.

Home hints

Grow rosemary in your borders or in tubs. Rosemary is a top choice for your garden according to experts who have discovered that the scent may help increase alertness and accuracy. This fragrant herb is hardy, evergreen and can be harvested all year round – we love it!

Wise words

"Have three of everything"
My lovely little Irish mum told me to always have 'one in use, one in stock and one in the wash' – great advice for everything from clothes to crockery.
Sally Ketley, Chelmsford

Headgear of yesteryear

I love this picture of my grandparents' wedding. Granddad looks very dapper and confident making his speech, and something has obviously made my grandma giggle! She looks very happy, and her navy blue feathered hat with the small veil looks so fashionable – much like the fascinators we wear to weddings these days. I also love my great-grandmother's 'pork pie' style hat – such a typical style of the time.
Rachel Chambers,
via email

Recipe of the week

Apple, Elderflower & Almond Pie

Serves: 8
Preparation time: 1 hour
Cooking time: 30 minutes

340g (12oz) plain flour
225g (8oz) butter
4 tbsp caster sugar
1 egg yolk
7 Pink Lady apples
250ml (9fl.oz) elderflower cordial
100ml (3 ½fl.oz) water
Zest of 1 lemon, finely grated
25g (1oz) ground almonds
115g (4oz) white marzipan
Flaked almonds, to top
Icing sugar, to dust

1 Process the flour and butter until the mixture resembles breadcrumbs. Add the caster sugar and process again. Now add the yolk and mix until your pastry comes together into a ball. Wrap in cling film and leave to rest in the fridge for 45 minutes or so.
2 Core and quarter the apples; peel them if you prefer. Cut each into slices, about 3mm (⅛in) thick. Put in a pan with the cordial and water, cover and simmer gently until the apples just begin to get tender. Strain off the liquid and measure it. If it is more than 75ml (3fl.oz) then boil to reduce it to that.
3 Stir in the zest, then pour the liquid over the apples and leave to cool. Preheat the oven to 190°C/375°F/Gas Mark 5.
4 Roll out ⅔ of the pastry and line a 25cm (10in) pie dish. Sprinkle the ground almonds over. Break the marzipan up into little chunks. Spoon the apples (with the elderflower syrup) into the pie, scattering marzipan as you go.
5 Roll out the rest of the pastry and make 6 strips for a lattice. Moisten each end and lay them across the top of the pie. Press to seal.
6 Bake for 30 minutes, or until golden. 8 minutes before the end, scatter over some flaked almonds, to toast. Dust with icing sugar before serving.
© Pink Lady Apples, www.pinkladyapples.co.uk

22 Monday

23 Tuesday

24 Wednesday

25 Thursday

26 Friday

27 Saturday

28 Sunday

Every picture tells a story

Like peas in a pod

These identical twins are Eileen and Vera Barrow. They were aged around eight or nine when this photo was taken in the early Thirties. Their father owned a bakery in Wimborne, Dorset, and they had quite a strict upbringing. The sisters were always exceptionally well dressed in identical outfits and were well known in the town.

When they grew up, both became hairdressers. Marriage separated them – Eileen lived with her husband in Eastbourne and Vera moved to London when she married my grandfather, but they remained close to the end of their lives.

My grandmother never went out without a beautiful outfit, make-up and her hair styled to perfection. She lived until she was 80 and I remember that even at that age she still looked as smart as paint and the height of fashion. Sadly, Eileen had died a few years before Vera who was devastated by the loss of her sister and best friend.

Nigel Hardy, Basingstoke

On this week...

September 23, 1952 – Little Tramp comes home
Comic actor Charlie Chaplin returned to his native England for the first time in 21 years. He arrived at Southampton on the Queen Elizabeth with wife Oona and their four children. Chaplin, the son of music hall entertainers, was born in London in 1889. At a press conference at the Savoy Hotel he said that Big Ben was 'a beautiful sight'.

Home hints

Keep old buttons as they come in useful for all sorts! Use them to decorate cushions, cards and anything crafty. Use them as earring holders – to keep both earrings safely together. Or, if you're feeling really crafty they can be made into earrings and necklaces. You can buy jewellery making kits from most craft shops.

Wise words

"God grant me the serenity to accept the things I cannot change...
...Courage to change the things I can and the wisdom to know the difference."
I have tried to live by the words of the serenity prayer, which my husband first read to me when I was working in America and finding the 'accepting' part a little difficult.

Sue Payne, Oxford

Headgear of yesteryear

This is a picture of my husband's mum, dad, grandma and granddad dated 1965. They are at Hastings Station in East Sussex.
Grandma and Granddad were on their way back to Durham after a two-week holiday at the seaside. They are all smiling for the camera but I expect the tears were not far away as they would not meet up again for another six months.

**Julie Vinsome,
Bognor Regis, West Sussex**

Recipe of the week

Autumnal Beef and Chestnut Casserole

Serves: 4
Preparation time: 25 minutes
Cooking time: 2 hours

450g (1lb) lean stewing or braising beef, cut into 2.5cm (1in) cubes
2 tbsp plain flour seasoned with salt and pepper
2 tsp ground nutmeg
2 tsp oil
8 shallots, peeled and left whole
2 garlic cloves, peeled and crushed
175g (6oz) baby carrots, topped and left whole
4 tomatoes, skinned, deseeded and roughly chopped
Zest of 1 lemon, grated
450ml ($^3/_4$pt) hot beef stock
200ml (7fl.oz) red wine
1 tbsp fresh thyme leaves
200g (7oz) cooked and peeled whole chestnuts
Mustard mash, to serve

1 Preheat the oven to 170°C/325°F/Gas Mark 3.
2 Place the flour, seasoning and nutmeg into a large plastic food bag. Add the beef in batches and coat with the seasoned flour.
3 Heat the oil in a non-stick frying pan and cook the beef for 4-5 minutes until brown on all sides. Transfer to an ovenproof casserole dish.
4 In the same frying pan, cook the shallots, garlic and carrots for 2-3 minutes. Spoon into the casserole dish with the tomatoes.
5 Add the remaining ingredients to the casserole dish, bring to the boil, cover and cook in the oven for 1 $^1/_2$-2 hours. Serve with mustard mash.

Top Tip: This is perfect cooked in a slow cooker, but always refer to the manufacturer's instructions.
© Simply Beef and Lamb, www.simplybeefandlamb.co.uk

29 Monday

30 Tuesday

1 Wednesday

2 Thursday

3 Friday

4 Saturday

5 Sunday

Every picture tells a story

A yoga yearning

When I was 46 years old, the thought suddenly dropped into my head, 'You have to teach yoga'. At that time I had never even been to a yoga class but the idea filled me with excitement. I enrolled on a course in Norwich with a lovely teacher.

When I told her why I was there she was very supportive. Every day I practised at home with a book in one hand as I read the instructions! When I felt ready, I enrolled on a teacher training correspondence course with the British School of Yoga and passed with flying colours. Since then I have studied and taught yoga in England and Spain as well as travelling to India where I learned how to apply yoga to one's everyday life.

This photo was taken of me beside the River Ganges in Rishikesh where I lived in an ashram for six weeks and studied yoga with an authentic Himalayan yogi.

Maggie Levien, Wymondham, Norfolk

On this week...

October 1, 1975 – Ali wins 'Thrilla in Manila'
Muhammad Ali beat his arch rival, British heavyweight Joe Frazier, in their third encounter in the ring. The fight lasted 14 rounds before Frazier's trainer finally persuaded him to throw in the towel. Some ringside commentators called it the greatest heavyweight title fight ever. Afterwards Ali said of his defeated rival: "I didn't realise he was so great. He's a real, real fighter."

Home hints

Start preparing for the colder months and make sure your heating is in good working order. Getting your boiler serviced is sensible and you may find the cost is lower if you get it done early. In winter the recommended temperature for your main living room is 21°C and at least 18°C for the rest of your house, including your bedroom.

Wise words

"Never let the sun go down on your anger"
Mum used to say this to us when we were young and made sure we kept to it. If we fell out as children she insisted that we make friends before we went to bed so we could start the next day afresh.

Gill Hughes, Northwich

Headgear of yesteryear

This photograph is of Aunt Peggy, taken in the late Twenties or early Thirties. She was a very glamorous lady and worked as Head Mannequin at a gown shop where she was employed, modelling the clothes. I have several photos of her, and most of her outfits could easily be worn today. I love this one, and think the lovely matching hat shows that she really knew how to put an outfit together.

A Gifford, Poole, Dorset

Recipe of the week

Triple Chocolate Marble Cake

Serves: 12
Preparation time: 30 minutes
Cooking time: 1 hour

225g (8oz) butter, softened
225g (8oz) fine Demerara sugar
4 large eggs
225g (8oz) self-raising flour
2 tbsp milk
1 tsp vanilla extract
2 tbsp cocoa powder
For the topping
150ml (5 ¼fl.oz) double cream
100g (3 ½oz) milk or dark chocolate
75g (3oz) white chocolate, melted

1 Preheat the oven to 180°C/350°F/Gas Mark 4. Grease a 20cm (8in) cake tin and line the bottom with a circle of greaseproof paper.
2 Beat the butter and sugar together, then add the eggs, one at a time, mixing well after each addition. Fold through the flour, milk and vanilla extract until the mixture is smooth.
3 Divide the mixture between 2 bowls. Stir the cocoa powder into one of the bowls. Add the chocolate and vanilla cake mixes to the tin alternately, until it all has been used up. Swirl the mixture a few times to create a marbled effect.
4 Bake for 50-60 minutes until a skewer inserted into the centre comes out clean. If the cake isn't ready after an hour, cover loosely with foil and return to the oven until cooked through. Turn out onto a rack and leave to cool.
5 For the ganache topping, heat the cream in a pan and bring to the boil, then take off the heat. Place the chocolate in a large bowl, pour over the cream and stir to melt. Allow to cool slightly; the mixture will thicken. Transfer the cake to a serving plate and pour the ganache over the top. Drizzle with melted white chocolate to decorate.
© Whitworths, www.whitworths-sugar.co.uk

6	Monday

7	Tuesday

8	Wednesday

9	Thursday

10	Friday

11	Saturday

12	Sunday

Every picture tells a story

Two role models

Two women were major influences in my life, my grandma (pictured) and my Aunt Lillian. As my mother was ill, my grandmother cared for me as a baby. She enjoyed cookery, gardening, keeping pets, embroidery and knitting and passed all these skills onto me. Family was a priority and she visited all her relatives regularly. In later life, she enjoyed watching sport on TV – as I do now.

My other role model, my aunt, had a small preparatory school called The Laurels which I attended from 1941. Despite the air-raids, she maintained strict discipline with an emphasis on teaching the three Rs (reading, writing and arithmetic), religious education and geography. We also learned to help others in need.

When I grew up and became a teacher myself I followed her teaching methods and encouraged my pupils to help others, especially the elderly.

Priscilla J Odell, Hampton

On this week...

October 7, 1977 – Swedish twins set sail for Britain
Ninety sets of identical twins from Sweden arrived in the port of Felixstowe for a 'shopping trip'. The twins were all taking part in a study by researchers from the Karolinska Institute in Stockholm. The shopping trip was organised by the captain of the ship they sailed in, who was himself a twin. The twins, aged from 11 to 80, were all wearing matching outfits.

Home hints

Place a saucer on your radiator and add a few drops of lavender essential oil. The heat will help disperse the scent around your home. Lavender is brilliant for helping you to relax ad sleep better, too.

Wise words

"Good times, bad times, all passes over"
These are the words my sister said to me when I was going through a rough patch in my life. How right she was and I've often had cause to remember them since.

Margaret Shearwood, Romford

Headgear of yesteryear

I was wearing this hat when I met my late husband during the war. He came into the pub where my friend and I were having a drink, and said how pretty the hat was. I was so pleased! These hats were very popular in the Forties and many of my friends had similar ones, but mine was handmade by a good friend who styled it just as I asked. This one was black with grey trim.

Norah Barber, Boston, Lincolnshire

Recipe of the week

Duck Breasts with Mandarin Marmalade Sauce

Serves: 2
Preparation time: 10 minutes
Cooking time: 25 minutes

2 duck breasts, about 175-225g (6-8oz) each, skin on and scored
2 tbsp freshly squeezed orange or mandarin juice
3 tbsp mandarin marmalade
1 tbsp olive oil
Salt and freshly ground pepper
Mixed rice with herbs, French beans and peas, to serve

1 Preheat the oven to 200°C/400°F/Gas Mark 6.
2 Heat a heavy pan without any fat for a few minutes until very hot. Add the duck breasts, skin side down, and cook for 5-6 minutes until the skin is crisp and golden brown.
3 Turn the breasts over and transfer them to a roasting tin. Place in the centre of the pre-heated oven and cook for about 10 minutes. Remove and leave to rest on a warm dish.
4 While the duck is resting, place the juice and the marmalade in a pan. Heat gently until the marmalade has melted and stir in the oil. Season to taste.
5 Slice the duck breasts diagonally, place on warm plates and pour over the marmalade sauce. Serve with mixed herby rice, French beans and peas.
© Bonne Maman, www.lovebonnemaman.co.uk

13 Monday

14 Tuesday

15 Wednesday

16 Thursday

17 Friday

18 Saturday

19 Sunday

Every picture tells a story

My first job

I left grammar school at the age of 16 with eight 'O' levels and got a job as a clerk at a branch of the Midland Bank opposite Westminster Abbey. The photo shows me (on the right, with a rose tucked into my neckline) with some of my colleagues.

I operated one of the branch's Burroughs accounting machines for which I was paid four guineas a week.

I gave my mother half of this for my keep and the rest went on fares, clothes and entertainment. To start work, my parents bought me two smart blouses and a black pencil skirt.

I thought I was the bees' knees with a chiffon scarf trailing from the pocket and black patent high heels. It was the year of the Queen's Coronation and the bank was ideally placed for a view of the procession, but places were limited so in the end I watched it on the TV at home.

**Pamela De La Touche,
Holbeach, Lincs**

On this week...

October 19, 2003 – Magician back on solid ground
Having spent 44 days suspended in a glass box by the River Thames in London, American illusionist and magician David Blaine was finally set free. His feat of endurance had attracted large crowds, with an estimated 10,000 people there to see him come out. Blaine took his first solid food in months – a handful of crisps – five days later.

Home hints

Treat your hair to a hair mask overnight once a week. Simply apply before bed, pop on a shower cap and hit the hay. Shampoo and condition as normal in the morning and then feel luscious locks that will be nicely nourished and less prone to breakages.

Wise words

"Always treat people the way you'd like to be treated"
My mother said this to me when I was a teenager and I have tried to live by it ever since. If everyone adopted it we'd live in a more considerate world.
Diane Clarke, Bristol

Headgear of yesteryear

This is my most precious photo of a hat. It's of me and my dad taken in 2003, when I graduated with a Certificate in Education at 52 years old. My graduation hat was special then, but more so now as my dad passed away in January 2013. This photo is on display in my living room so I can still see my dad looking so happy and know how very proud he was on that day.
Brenda Kenny, via email

Recipe of the week

Blueberry, Coconut and Lime Squares

Makes: 16
Preparation time: 20 minutes
Cooking time: 30-35 minutes

60g (2oz) desiccated coconut
150g (5 ¼) punnet fresh blueberries, rinsed
40g (1 ¾oz) plain flour
175g (6oz) self-raising flour
1tsp baking powder
175g (6oz) caster sugar
175g (6oz) unsalted butter, softened
3 medium eggs, beaten
Grated rind and juice of 2 large limes
100g (3 ½oz) caster sugar

1 Preheat the oven to 180°C/350°F/Gas Mark 4, and lightly grease and line a 23cm (9in) square baking tin.
2 In a small bowl mix together 50g of the coconut, the blueberries and plain flour and set aside.
3 Sift together the self-raising flour and baking powder into a mixing bowl with the caster sugar, butter and eggs. Whisk together until the sponge is well blended. Stir in the grated lime and fold in the coconut and blueberry mix. Spoon into the prepared tin and smooth over the surface of the sponge mixture.
4 Bake for 30-35 minutes until risen, or when a skewer comes out clean. Remove the sponge from the oven and set aside to cool.
5 While the cake is still warm, mix together the lime juice, remaining coconut and caster sugar. Using a skewer, prick the sponge all over and drizzle the sweetened lime juice over the surface of the cake. Cut into squares and serve warm or cold.

Top Tip: You can use any soft berry fruits, such as raspberries or blackberries – they all contrast well with the lime.
© Flour Advisory Bureau, www.fabflour.co.uk

20	Monday
21	Tuesday
22	Wednesday
23	Thursday
24	Friday
25	Saturday
26	Sunday

Every picture tells a story

One big happy family

I love this photo because it brings back happy memories of a carefree childhood. It was taken on a rare day out at Billing Aquadrome in 1965. The six girls are all cousins (our mothers were five sisters) and the solemn-looking little girl at the front with a big bow in her hair is me. Note the neat white ankle socks we are all wearing! In those days large extended families were not as unusual as they are now.

We grew up in adjoining streets and played together. Our mothers helped each other out with bringing us up and there was always someone to turn to when problems arose. But, sadly, times have changed and although we all still live in the same area, we seldom see each other these days as we all have our busy lives.

Kate Hardy, Kettering, Northants

On this week...

October 24, 2003 – Concorde's last flight
Supersonic airplane Concorde landed at the end of its last commercial flight to be greeted by emotional scenes at Heathrow. One hundred celebrities were aboard the flight, which ended 27 years of supersonic history. Actress Joan Collins, who had flown on Concorde about ten times, said the end of the era was 'tragic', but sadly the super-fast planes were no longer profitable.

Home hints

If you've added a bit too much salt to that stew you've been slaving over all afternoon try adding a raw peeled potato, cook for 15 minutes before removing. Too spicy? Add a squirt of honey. Too sweet? Add a drop of vinegar.

Wise words

"Strength for today and bright hope for tomorrow"
A few years ago I was going through a difficult patch and a caring work colleague said these words to me. Every day I recited them to myself and slowly I came through the turmoil. I later found out they were from the hymn Great Is Thy Faithfulness.

Name withheld

Headgear of yesteryear

I love this photo of my two nans at mum and dad's wedding. It's the only picture I have of the two of them together. On the right is mum's mum, Alice Wiltshire, who sadly I never got to meet because she died before I was born. On the other hand dad's mum, Jessie, was always close by when we were growing up. Quite a few people in the wedding album are wearing similar creations.

Sharon Palmer,
Peterborough, Cambridgeshire

Recipe of the week

Cajun Chicken Bake with Pineapple Salsa

Serves: 4
Preparation time: 10 minutes
Cooking time: 30 minutes

4 medium potatoes, cut into wedges
4 chicken breasts, cut into chunks
2tbsp Cajun spice mix (or mix 1tsp each of smoked paprika, dried oregano, ground black pepper, dried thyme and $1/2$ tsp chilli powder)
100g (3 $1/2$oz) baby sweetcorn
1 onion, peeled and cut into wedges
For the Pineapple Salsa
227g (8oz) tinned pineapple, drained and roughly chopped
1 green pepper, deseeded and finely chopped
Pinch chilli flakes

1 Preheat oven to 200°C/400°F/Gas Mark 6.
2 Place all ingredients (except salsa ingredients) onto a large baking tray. Toss together to coat all the ingredients. Spread out into one single layer.
3 Place in oven and cook for about 30 minutes, until browned and tender.
4 Mix together the ingredients for the Salsa and serve with the Cajun bake.
© Potato Council, www.manyfacesofpotatoes.co.uk

27	Monday

28	Tuesday

29	Wednesday

30	Thursday

31	Friday

1	Saturday

2	Sunday

Every picture tells a story

Away from home

During the war, I was evacuated from Plymouth to Cornwall with my sister, Mary, and my aunt, also called Mary, who was only a few years older than we were.

We were accompanied by my gran who was to be our guardian. Our new home was Glen Cottage in the village of Pencuke, near Bude.

We all felt very sad about leaving the rest of the family but after a while we got settled in to our new life and started to explore the glorious countryside around us.

We all slept in one bedroom and even though we were far away from the bombing, Gran insisted that we go to bed wearing our Wellingtons and overcoats just in case there was a stray bomb.

Once a fortnight we had a parcel from mum in which she put her saved-up sweet coupons, broken biscuits and anything else she could find to fill it up.

Liz Jones,
Plymouth, Devon

On this week...

October 30, 1957 – Lords admits female peers
Conservative Leader of the House, Lord Home, announced proposals to create both male and female life peerages in order to bring about a balance of both sexes in the House of Lords. Welcoming the amendment, Liberal peer Lord Samuel said reform had come about through 'elephantine deliberations'. In 1958 the Life Peerages Act empowered the Crown to create female life peers for the first time.

Home hints

Get your bulbs ready for spring. If you haven't got round to planting your spring-flowering bulbs, don't just leave them in the shed. Spring bulbs need to spend some time in the soil when the cold weather hits so they can sprout next season. Pop them in pots with lots of soil so they are well insulated and store in the shed where it's cold.

Wise words

"People are lonely because they build walls instead of bridges"
I don't recall where I first heard these wise words but I have found it to be true over the years.

Margaret Nicol, Glasgow

Headgear of yesteryear

This photograph was taken in 1947. I was 20 years old and used to pass a milliner on my way to work as a secretary. I was fascinated by her creations – after the austerity of the war years, things were getting a bit more glamorous, and Peggy's hat shop was very popular. Mother had just made me the green tweed coat and this brown hat was a 'must-have'!

Margery Sagar, Sheffield, South Yorkshire

Recipe of the week

Roasted Pumpkin, Leek and Ginger Soup with Pastry Tops

Serves: 6
Preparation time: 30 minutes
Cooking time: 50 minutes

500g (1lb 1 ½oz) All butter puff pastry, thawed
1.5kg (3lb) pumpkin, peeled and sliced medium-thick
3 large leeks, trimmed and washed
4cm (1 ½in) root ginger, peeled and cut into matchsticks
4 tbsp olive oil
500ml (17 ½fl.oz) chicken or vegetable stock
150g (5 ¼oz) Lancashire cheese
Beaten egg, to glaze
Salt and black pepper

1 Preheat oven to 200°C/400°F/Gas Mark 6.
2 Cut the slices of pumpkin into 7 cm (2 ½in) lengths, and the leeks in half lengthways then in similar lengths. Arrange all vegetables and ginger on a heavy baking tray, drizzle with the oil and roast for approx. 20 minutes until just tender.
3 Remove from oven and place half the vegetables in a blender with the stock. Blend until smooth and season to taste. Allow to cool along with the remaining vegetables which you should cut into smaller chunks.
4 Increase oven heat to 220°C/425°F/Gas Mark 7 and have ready 6 ovenproof bowls.
5 Divide pastry into 6 and roll out each piece large enough to cover the tops of the soup bowls. Divide soup and chunks between dishes, then crumble in some of the cheese. Brush rims of the dishes with beaten egg.
6 Top dishes with pastry, pressing well at edges to seal. Brush the tops with beaten egg, make a small hole in centre and then sprinkle with grated cheese. Bake for 18-20 minutes, until pastry is risen and golden brown.
© Jus-Rol, www.jusrol.co.uk

3   Monday

4   Tuesday

5   Wednesday

6   Thursday

7   Friday

8   Saturday

9   Sunday

Every picture tells a story

An artistic family

This is a painting I did of my daughter's cat, Paddy. My lifelong interest in art was inspired by my Aunt Jean who used to take me round the London art galleries and museums in the holidays when I was a teenager.

She was an artist herself and specialised in paintings of flowers which were exhibited at the Royal Academy. One of the early women students at King's College, London, she went on to teach botany and biology.

Aunt Jean encouraged me to admire all the Old Masters as well: Monet, Renoir and Vermeer. I took art as one of my main subjects when I went to teachers' training college in the Fifties.

These days I paint animal portraits in oils and watercolours and receive many commissions to paint people's dogs and horses. Cats are more of a challenge as they refuse to sit still for long!

**Oonagh M Gleeson,
Needham Market, Suffolk**

On this week...

November 3, 1975 – North Sea oil starts to flow
The Queen officially opened the UK's first oil pipeline in the small Scottish town of Dyce near Aberdeen. The 130-mile pipeline was expected to produce about one fifth of the country's oil. It was the first time a party of royals and high-ranking officials had visited Dyce. Despite fears that proceedings would be disrupted by Scottish republicans – the so-called Tartan Army – the ceremony passed peacefully.

Home hints

Eat butternut squash. They are packed full of nutrients called carotenoids and vitamins A and C are a great source of fibre – essential for keeping your digestive system healthy. It's also a source of antioxidants and has anti-inflammatory benefits. The seeds make a great snack, too. Simply roast in the oven for 15 minutes.

Wise words

"Look after your feet as well as you do your face"
A neighbour gave me this sage advice when I was just 23 years old. I took heed of her words and I'm so glad I did, after all they support you throughout your life.

Ann West, Bowdon

Headgear of yesteryear

This is a photo of my wife, Patricia, in a hat she won in 1984. The competition was in a national daily newspaper and the prize was a replica of a designer hat made for and worn by Diana, Princess of Wales. A friend, who was a member of the local photographic club, took this great picture. Although it was nearly 30 years ago Pat still has the hat – and she's still as lovely as ever.

R Thompson, Pontyclun, Rhondda Cynon Taf

Recipe of the week

Bonfire Night Parkin

Makes: 16
Preparation time: 15 minutes
Cooking time: 1 hour 15 minutes, plus cooling

100g (3 ^{1}/$_2$oz) butter
100g (3 ^{1}/$_2$oz) black treacle
200g (7oz) golden syrup
100g (3 ^{1}/$_2$oz) dark brown muscovado sugar
200g (7oz) self-raising flour
2 tsp ground ginger
^{1}/$_2$ tsp ground cinnamon
1 tsp bicarbonate of soda
100g (3 ^{1}/$_2$oz) medium oatmeal
1 egg, beaten
6 tbsp milk

1 Preheat the oven to 150°C/300°F/Gas mark 2. Grease and line a 20cm (8in) square cake tin with baking parchment. Heat the butter in a pan with the treacle, syrup and sugar over a low heat until all melted together. Remove from the heat and allow to cool slightly.
2 Sieve the flour with the ginger, cinnamon and bicarbonate of soda into a large mixing bowl, then stir in the oatmeal. Make a well in the centre and gradually add the cooled syrup mixture, stirring and taking care that it doesn't become lumpy. Stir in the beaten egg and milk, to resemble the consistency of thick batter.
3 Pour into the prepared tin and cook for 1-1 ^{1}/$_4$ hours, until just firm to the touch. Leave in the tin to cool completely – it will sink in the middle). Remove from the tin and cut into pieces.

Top tip: Cook a few days in advance, and store in an airtight tin – for up to a week, if you can wait! – as parkin can go hard to begin with but should then soften.
© Over 5,000 recipes at www.waitrose.com

10	Monday
11	Tuesday
12	Wednesday
13	Thursday
14	Friday
15	Saturday
16	Sunday

Every picture tells a story

Glamorous nanny

This photo was taken when I was nanny to these three adorable children, Victoria, Vickie and Edward, who lived in Shaftesbury Avenue in London. They were very well behaved and I loved them dearly. Edward wouldn't smile for the camera as he had just lost his milk teeth and didn't want to reveal the gap. My 'ringlet' hairstyle was considered very chic in the Fifties.

After my three years as a nanny, I returned to my home town of Chesham where I won the title of Miss Chesham three years running and went on to win 12 other beauty queen titles at seaside resorts such as Clapton and Ramsgate. It was around this time that I met my husband-to-be, Donald. He moved in to the house next door and we got talking while picking beans in the garden! We now have two grandchildren and one great grandchild.

Rose Whitehead, Chalfont St Peter, Bucks

Home hints

Avoid drying your hair straight after washing. Gently towel dry and leave to dry slightly. Using high heat on very wet hair creates steam, which can damage the hair surface and lead to dull hair that's prone to breakages.

Wise words

"Don't judge a man by the colour of his skin but the contents of his heart"
Taken from Martin Luther King's 'I have a dream' speech these are the words that I try to live by.
Jean Sallabank, Bristol

Headgear of yesteryear

This is a photo of my father, Victor Spencer. It was taken just before he joined the Army in the First World War, when he would have been 23. I love the hat and smart bow tie! He would have been working in his father's shoe shop in Bishop Stortford at the time this was taken. He was an ordinary, happy gent who was loved by everyone around him.
Ruth Spencer, Maidstone, Kent

On this week...

November 16, 1960 – 'Rudest man on television' dies
TV personality Gilbert Harding, renowned for his outspoken and sometimes rude behaviour, died after collapsing with a heart attack outside the BBC's Broadcasting House. Harding, a Cambridge graduate, was a regular panellist on What's My Line?. Before working in television, he had a variety of careers including policeman, teacher and Times correspondent in Cyprus.

Recipe of the week

Smoked Haddock and Broccoli Filo Pie

Serves: 6
Preparation time: 20 minutes
Cooking time: 25 minutes

4 filo pastry sheets, thawed
350g (12 $^{1}/_{4}$oz) broccoli, cut into florets
450g (1lb) smoked haddock, skinned and cut or torn into chunks
50g (2oz) butter, melted
300g (10 $^{1}/_{2}$oz) jar lemon & dill sauce
Few sprigs parsley, chopped

1 Preheat oven to 190°C/ 375°F/Gas Mark 5.
2 Blanch broccoli in boiling salted water, drain and refresh under cold water, and drain again. Place broccoli and haddock in base of a shallow ovenproof dish and spoon over sufficient sauce to coat lightly.
3 Add half the chopped parsley to the melted butter, and lightly brush one filo sheet. Tear pastry roughly into 4 strips and loosely fold or drape over fish filling, continuing with remaining pastry until all filling is covered.
4 Scatter with a little more chopped parsley and bake for approximately 25 minutes, until pastry is golden and the filling bubbling. Serve with any remaining sauce.
© Jus-Rol, www.jusrol.co.uk

17 Monday

18 Tuesday

19 Wednesday

20 Thursday

21 Friday

22 Saturday

23 Sunday

Every picture tells a story

Early learning

My primary school headmistress made a lasting impression on me. She was always firm but never nasty.

We feared yet respected her. In winter she made us run around the annexe to get warm and anyone who dared to say they were still cold was made to run around again. She taught us everything from swimming to country dancing.

I remember chanting our times tables aloud to learn them. She encouraged us to do our homework – although with my dad's help with maths, I frequently got it wrong! At Christmas, I was always made an angel in the nativity play.

Once, when I fell over and skinned both my knees, she dressed them in thick bandages. She even explained a funny way to remember how to do tricky embroidery stitches. She was a one-off and I remember her a lot these days as a gran to Melody (pictured).

Rosemary Medland, Hitchin

On this week...

November 18, 1983 – Six beautiful babies
Britain's first surviving sextuplets, all girls, were born in Liverpool to Graham and Janet Walton. The couple had been trying for a baby for five years and conceived with spectacular results on their 13th round of fertility treatment. The girls arrived at 31 weeks and were all born within four minutes of each other.

Home hints

Make your diamonds sparkle with washing up liquid. Always do this in a bowl out of the kitchen sink, to avoid losing your valuables down the plughole! Use a soft or baby toothbrush to gently scrub into those nooks and crannies. Rinse well to finish and use a chamois leather to buff.

Wise words

"You can't change someone else's behaviour, but you can change your reaction"
This is the best piece of advice I've ever been given – I just wish I'd heard it many years ago because it would have saved me a lot of heartache.

Sue Wilding, Scarborough

Headgear of yesteryear

Being the youngest of nine children, seven of them girls, 'Secondhand Rose' was an understatement! This is me in my first all new outfit, complete with hat, aged 14 in 1954. The hat was grey, and the coat was light grey with yellow checks. I paid each week into a group, and your turn came every so often to go and have your photo taken, which was a lovely idea.

Joyce Whalley, Wigan, Lancashire

Recipe of the week

Cauliflower Cheese with Saffron and Gremolata Crumbs

Serves: 4-6
Preparation time: 25 minutes
Cooking time: 35-45 minutes

2 small cauliflowers, chopped
1.2l (2pt) milk
Pinch saffron
30g (1oz) butter
30g (1oz) plain flour
350g (12 ¼oz) cheddar cheese, grated
2 egg yolks, beaten
For the Gremolata Crumbs
30g (1oz) unsalted butter
100g (3 ½oz) fresh white breadcrumbs
Finely grated zest of 1 lemon
2 small garlic cloves, finely chopped
4 tbsp chopped fresh parsley
Salt and freshly ground black pepper

1 Blanch the cauliflower in a large pan of salted boiling water until just tender. Drain, then place in an ovenproof dish. Preheat oven to 200°C/400°F/ Gas Mark 6.
2 Pour the milk into a large pan, add the saffron and bring to just below boiling point. Remove from heat and set aside.
3 Melt the butter in another pan over medium heat. Turn down the heat slightly and add the flour. Stir continuously for 1-2 minutes. Pour in some milk and beat to a creamy consistency. Gradually continue adding, beating well, for a thick, smooth sauce.
4 Take the pan off the heat, season with salt and pepper and stir in ³/₄ of the cheese and the egg yolks. Mix until the cheese has melted. Pour over the cauliflower, sprinkle on the remaining cheese and cook in the oven for 35-45 minutes, until golden and bubbling.
5 Meanwhile, melt the remaining butter in a frying pan over a medium heat. Add the breadcrumbs and stir occasionally, until golden and crisp. Remove from heat and cool slightly, before stirring in the lemon zest, garlic and parsley. Scatter over cauliflower to serve.

© Davidstow Cheddar, www.davidstowcheddar.co.uk

24 Monday

25 Tuesday

26 Wednesday

27 Thursday

28 Friday

29 Saturday

30 Sunday

Every picture tells a story

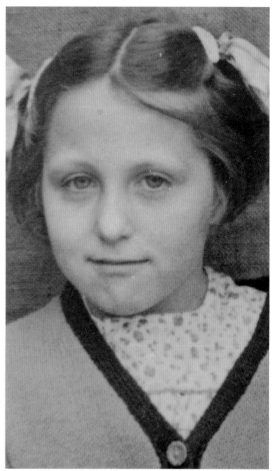

Fun and games

Where I grew up, in Wimbledon, there were quite a few parks which could be used for different types of games. Near our flat in Haydons Road, there was one with a bandstand.

This was used by us as a fort, a castle, a boat or a house. Another park had swings and slides at one end and a recreation ground at the other end for weekend football matches. We often went to the pictures on Saturday mornings.

Wimbledon high street had two cinemas directly opposite each other. We would queue outside and shout across to each other that we had Flash Gordon or Roy Rogers on and try to get them to come to our side.

If any children did cross over the road there were loud cheers from us and boos from the others. You could always tell what films we had seen by our antics when we came out.

**Hazel Miller,
Blandford Forum, Dorset**

Home hints

Spare a thought for your skin and hair, as chilly winter weather can cause lots of damage. Treat both to a moisturising boost with coconut oil. Use it as an intensive conditioner by massaging it into your hair, leave to soak for ten minutes then rinse, or massage it into your skin straight after the bath. You can even cook with it!

Wise words

"Forgive, forgive, forgive"
My dear old dad said this to me when I was angry one day. He was such a lovely, kind and clever man. I keep remembering his words, especially when faced with family squabbles.

Celia Preston, Leicester

Headgear of yesteryear

My granddaughter, Rachel, looks so cute in this woolly bonnet! I think this would have been taken when she was about three years old, in 1978, outside our local church. I doubt she could read the hymnbook she seems to be carrying, but at least she seems interested! I love how cosy she looks – even now she doesn't like the cold and loves to be wrapped up warm!

Sheila Barker, Wakefield, West Yorkshire

On this week...

November 28, 1971 – Farmer foils drug smugglers
A Cambridgeshire farmer became a hero after ramming a plane used by drug smugglers. Detectives had asked Ray Convine to keep an eye on a disused wartime airfield on his land after a tip off. Convine drove alongside the plane after it landed then rammed his truck into its side. The ringleader handed himself in shortly afterwards.

Recipe of the week

Scottish Tea Loaf

Makes: 1 loaf
Preparation time: 20 minutes, plus overnight soaking
Cooking time: 50 minutes, plus 5 minutes cooling

450g (1lb) mixed dried fruits
250g (9oz) soft light brown sugar
200ml (7fl.oz) cold tea
2 tsp Scotch whisky
450g (1lb) self-raising flour
1 tsp mixed spice
1 egg, beaten

1 Mix together the dried fruit and sugar and pour over the cold tea and whisky (whisky is optional, you can use just tea if you prefer, but it does give a lovely depth of flavour), cover the bowl and leave to soak overnight.
2 Preheat the oven to 190°C/375°F/Gas Mark 5 and line a 2lb loaf tin with greased baking paper.
3. Uncover your bowl and you will find that the fruit is beautifully swollen and juicy now. Sift the flour and spice into the fruit and stir well to combine. Now add the beaten egg and mix it all thoroughly.
4 Spoon the mixture into the prepared tin and bake for 50 minutes, or until a skewer comes out clean. If the cake is browning on top, place a piece of folded baking paper on top to protect it.
5 Let the cake cool in its tin for about 5 minutes and then take it out and let it cool thoroughly on a wire rack.

Top Tip: This is a two-part cake and you need to start things off the night before you want to bake it.
© Karon Grieve, www.karongrieve.com

December 1 - 7

1 Monday

2 Tuesday

3 Wednesday

4 Thursday

5 Friday

6 Saturday

7 Sunday

Every picture tells a story

A red carpet day

This photo was taken in 1949 at the Princess Margaret Rose school for girls in Windsor. There was great excitement as our patron, Princess Margaret, came to the school for prize-giving day.

I was in the fourth form and those of us who weren't receiving a prize performed a sort of gipsy dance as part of the entertainment.

We practised for weeks in advance and I remember the teacher walking round with a big stopwatch to make sure we got the timing absolutely right.

Much to our girlish amusement, the preparations for our royal visitor included putting a red carpet down in the toilets. At one point during the afternoon, I stood quite close to the Princess and was able to see that she was tiny, very pretty and had lovely blue eyes.

**Kathleen St John,
Hythe, Kent**

On this week...

December 7, 1983 – Moggy halts Dibnah's work
A ginger tomcat called George hit the headlines after foiling steeplejack Fred Dibnah's attempts to topple a 160 ft (49 m) industrial chimney. After an emergency meeting between the fire brigade, the RSPCA and Fred, it was decided to wait and see if George would come down on his own after a night without food. George was finally captured after a 30-hour stand-off.

Home hints

Winter can be a quiet time in the garden, but there are still jobs to be done. Now's a good time to prune apple and pear trees as well as shrub rose bushes. Cut away any diseased branches and thin out overcrowding. You still have time to plant deciduous trees and some shrubs. Don't forget to harvest any remaining parsnips.

Wise words

"I cried because I had no shoes, then I met a man with no feet"
I think this is an ancient proverb but my dad frequently said it to me and my brother and sister whenever we wanted something we couldn't have, either because they couldn't afford it or it wasn't necessary.

Sarah Downham, Blackburn

Headgear of yesteryear

This is a photo of my mother in a hat that always turned heads when she wore it. I guess it would have been taken in the Forties. We left Singapore, where my father was serving in the Army, in 1942 when the Japanese landed – our cargo ship was one of the last to get away. Unfortunately, my mother died young at 57 – how I wish my three children could have known their grandmother.

Sheila Evans, Epsom Downs, Surrey

Recipe of the week

Pan-fried Turkey with Carrots, Lime, Ginger and Coriander

Serves: 4
Preparation time: 10 minutes, plus 1–2 hours marinating
Cooking time: 15 minutes, plus 15–20 minutes for mash

4 turkey escalopes, 125g (4 1/2oz) each
250g (8 3/4oz) carrots, cut into small batons
For the marinade
1 clove garlic, finely chopped
1 tbsp ginger, finely chopped
2 tbsp dark soy sauce
2 tbsp vegetable or groundnut oil
1 tbsp sesame oil
Juice of 3 limes
1 tbsp sweet chilli sauce
2 tbsp chopped coriander
A little oil, for frying
Serving suggestion
Mashed potato
Lime slices, fried, to garnish

1 Marinate the escalopes for 1–2hrs then fry them in a little oil. Season with salt and pepper. Retain the marinade.
2 Stir fry the carrots in another pan and when they are soft add the chopped coriander and a little of the remaining marinade. Remove from the heat and keep warm.
3 Add the carrots and marinade to the turkey and keep hot. Serve with mashed potato and add some quickly fried lime slices to garnish.

Top tip: Cook and mash your potatoes towards the end of the marinating time, and keep hot – that way you can concentrate on the stir fry.
© Great British Carrots, www.britishcarrots.co.uk

December 8 - 14

8 Monday

9 Tuesday

10 Wednesday

11 Thursday

12 Friday

13 Saturday

14 Sunday

Every picture tells a story

The wild West Midlands

I was always a bit of a tomboy and here I am, aged around ten, playing cowboys and indians with my cousin (in the cowboy hat) and a neighbour's son. I had a brother and sister, but they were both quite a few years older than me.

We lived in Great Barr, a suburb of Birmingham and my father worked at Fisher & Ludlow which manufactured car parts for the mini.

We children used to race up and down the gulley that ran between the backs of the houses. Other games included kick the can which we played out in the street.

When you kicked a tin can, all the other children scattered to find a hiding place. Hopscotch on the pavement was another game I often played. I had a wonderful childhood that included a holiday every year to Wales or Cornwall, which is where I now live.

Chris Davies, Wadebridge, Cornwall

On this week...

December 10, 1979 – Biker Eddie's river leap
Motorcycle stuntman Eddie Kidd survived a death-defying 8oft leap over the River Blackwater at Maldon, Essex. Kidd, who was only 20 at the time, reached a speed of 100mph before soaring over a sheer 5oft drop. Afterwards he said: "I never want to do a jump like that again." Kidd went on to have more success until his career ended abruptly following an accident in 1996.

Home hints

Raid the fridge. No more moisturiser and you don't have time to get to the shops? Then natural yoghurt is a great alternative. It's nice and gentle and the lactic acid it contains has an exfoliating and refreshing action on your skin.

Wise words

"Anxiety doesn't empty tomorrow of its sorrows, but empties today of its strength"
I realised that I was spending too much time worrying when I came across this quote from Charles Spurgeon, a baptist minister. I find that it really helps me.

Tracy Munden, Spalding

Headgear of yesteryear

This photo was taken at Trent Bridge, Nottingham, with me in the middle and friends either side. This was the height of fashion for us and we thought we were the bees' knees, as you can tell from our swagger! I was undergoing initial officer training at RAF Cranwell and to be 'properly dressed' in civilian attire, officers would wear a hat. I was home on a week's leave when this photo was taken.

Geoffrey Starr, Doncaster, South Yorkshire

Recipe of the week

Mini Christmas Pudding Bites
Makes: About 20
Preparation time: 40 minutes

For the cakes
675g (1lb8oz) leftover cake – different cakes will vary end results
100g (3¹/₂oz) mincemeat
50g (2oz) chopped mixed nuts
50g (2oz) cocoa powder
25g (1oz) crystallised ginger
1 tsp natural almond extract
2 tbsp orange juice
2 tbsp brandy
For the topping
200g (7oz) white chocolate chips, melted
To decorate
Ready-to-roll green icing
Ready-to-roll red icing
Icing sugar, to dust
Small holly cutter (optional)

1 Crumble your leftover cake into a basin and add the remaining 'cake' ingredients. Add sufficient liquid to give a moist yet firm consistency.
2 Take a tablespoon of mixture at a time and roll into bite-sized balls. Place on a clean baking tray and refrigerate for 20 minutes.
3 Meanwhile, melt the white chocolate chips over a pan of simmering water until smooth. Allow to cool. Remove the puddings from the refrigerator and use a teaspoon to gently top each pudding with chocolate.
4 Knead the green icing, on a clean work surface lightly dusted with icing sugar, and roll out thinly. Stamp out holly shapes using a cutter, or create your own with a sharp tool. Place on a piece of crinkled aluminium foil to firm.
5 Position holly leaves on top of each pudding and allow to set. Finish by creating the holly berries. Take three small pieces of red icing and roll into very small balls to make berries. Set between the leaves.
© Mich Turner for Dr. Oetker, www.oetker.co.uk.

December 15 - 21

15 Monday

16 Tuesday

17 Wednesday

18 Thursday

19 Friday

20 Saturday

21 Sunday

Every picture tells a story

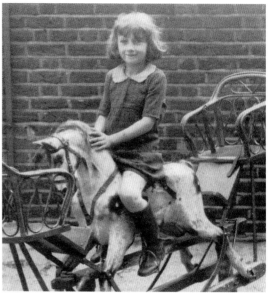

A pearly princess

This photo was taken of me in the schoolyard in the East End of London where I grew up. I loved school but, looking back, I suppose I was rather 'a little madam' and always played the fool.

I was often to be found standing outside the head's office waiting for the cane on my knuckles – at which I usually laughed, and got one more!

My dad was the Pearly King of Hackney and at Christmas he would go along to the local pub and bring home a couple of boys who were away from home, to share our turkey with all the trimmings (our once-a-year treat).

My memories are of a big crackling fire, chocolate 'double six' bars, nuts and oranges, and singing – which we all loved – while dad played on an old organ. We each had one toy, often made by dad, who was very clever with his hands. It was a wonderful time.

Joan Macdonald, Beckenham, Kent

On this week...

December 15, 1974 – New speed limits imposed
Britain's motorists were ordered to comply with new, lower speed limits in order to conserve fuel. At the time, there was a single 70mph speed limit on all roads. The 70mph motorway speed limit remained unchanged, but the speed limit was reduced to 60mph on dual carriageways and 50mph on all other roads. The aim was to reduce fuel imports after the price of oil rose sharply.

Home hints

Make your Christmas gifts even more special by adding a few festive finishing touches. Wrap them in brown parcel paper, which is relatively cheap, but provides a great base for extra decoration. Tie them with string or pretty ribbon and use natural elements such as cinnamon sticks, pinecones and dried fruits to decorate.

Wise words

"You can always learn – even from a bad experience"

I can't remember who told me this but it is so true. In fact, I've come to realise that it's life's worst experiences that teach you the most and that it is by coping that you learn to be stronger.

Rosie Turner, Brighton

Headgear of yesteryear

This is my daughter's Great-Granddad, Ray Scott, with his parents, Olive and Walter, as a baby in 1925. Hats were very much a part of life then and you weren't considered properly dressed unless you had one. Now aged 88, Great-Granddad Ray is always impeccably dressed, and is never seen without a suit and tie, and a hat. His wife often refers to him as her OEG (Old English Gentleman).

Kate Hardy, Kettering, Northamptonshire

Recipe of the week

Chocolate Reindeer Cupcakes

Serves: 12
Preparation time: 20 minutes
Cooking time: 25 minutes

125g (4 ¹/₂oz) butter, softened
150g (5 ¹/₄oz) caster sugar
2 free range eggs
200g (7oz) self-raising flour
2 tbsp cocoa powder
100g (3 ¹/₂oz) Greek yoghurt
100g (3 ¹/₂oz) dark chocolate, melted

For the topping
3 tbsp Greek yoghurt
50g (2oz) dark chocolate, melted

To decorate
Giant chocolate buttons
Smarties or similar
Mini pretzels
Mini marshmallows, sliced

1 Preheat the oven to 170°C/325°F/Gas Mark 3. Line a 12-hole muffin tin with paper cases.
2 Cream the butter and sugar together until light and fluffy. Beat in the eggs until well combined, sift in the flour and cocoa and mix.
3 Fold in the yoghurt and melted chocolate.
4 Spoon the mixture into the cases evenly and bake for 20-25 minutes until well risen. Remove from the oven and leave to cool.
5 To make the topping, mix the yoghurt into the melted chocolate. Spread over the cupcakes. Save a little and put into a small piping bag.
6 Press the chocolate buttons on to the cake to make a nose, then stick on the Smarties using topping from the piping bag. Stick on slices of marshmallow for eyes and dot with the topping. Finally, stick on pretzels to make ears.

© Total, www.totalgreekyoghurt.com

22 Monday

23 Tuesday

24 Wednesday

25 Thursday

26 Friday

27 Saturday

28 Sunday

Every picture tells a story

Tinsel time

Every year, after the Christmas tree had been decorated and the parcels piled around the bottom, my mother took a photo of the festive scene. As a family, we moved house often but the Christmas decorations always came with us and provided a sort of continuity against an ever-changing background.

There were fragile glass birds that dated from our time in Germany and flashing coloured lights we'd bought in Singapore. Mum usually made a fairy for the top of the tree, dressed in white tissue paper with a lop-sided tinsel crown.

On Twelfth Night, she took down all the precious baubles, wrapped them in tissue paper and put them in a box ready for the next Christmas – and the next house! As this photo shows, I have kept up the tradition with my own collection of decorations that I can't resist adding to each year.

Jackie Price, Newcastle Emlyn, Ceridigion

Home hints

Restore sparkle. Dishwashers are a godsend – especially at this time of year. Unfortunately, if you forget to keep the salt and rinse aid topped up you could find it leaves your glassware cloudy and dull. To try and restore that sparkle, soak them in warm white vinegar before scrubbing them with traditional white toothpaste.

Wise words

"Never buy cheap eggs or cheap tea – it's false economy!"
These are the wise words that my nan chose to share with my mum on her wedding day. I've always remembered them.   **Kate Paton, Huddersfield**

Headgear of yesteryear

Born in 1943, when most kids wore hand-me-downs from older siblings, I was an only child and fortunate in having a wonderful godmother who made all my clothes, from winceyette nightdresses to daytime and outdoor clothes. I loved this beret and coat, which was rust-coloured with a dark brown velvet collar. I felt a million dollars wearing such a wonderful matching outfit.

Jackie Hamblin, Newport, Isle of Wight

On this week...

December 25, 1952 – Queen's first Christmas speech
Millions of people in Britain and around the Commonwealth tuned in to hear a young Queen Elizabeth II make her first Christmas address. The message was retransmitted over the following days for those unable to get a good reception on Christmas Day. During the recording she used the same desk and chair at Sandringham as her father, King George VI, and grandfather, King George V, had used.

Recipe of the week

Last-minute Christmas Cake

Serves: 12
Preparation time: 20 minutes
Cooking time: 2-2 ½ hours

675g (1 ½lb) mixed dried fruits
75g (3oz) glacé cherries, quartered
Zest and juice of 1 lemon
Zest and juice of 1 orange
4 tbsp dark rum or brandy
225g (8oz) butter, softened
225g (8oz) light soft brown sugar
4 large British Lion eggs, beaten
225g (8oz) plain flour
½ tsp mixed ground spice
½ tsp ground cinnamon
50g (2oz) flaked almonds
To decorate
4 tbsp apricot jam, sieved
22 walnut halves
20 blanched almonds

1 Place the first four ingredients in a medium pan. Bring to the boil. Remove from the heat and stir in the rum or brandy; allow to cool.
2 Preheat the oven to 170°C/320°F/Gas Mark 3. Grease a 20cm (8in) deep, round cake tin and line with baking parchment.
3 Purée one third of the fruit in a processor.
4 Cream the butter and sugar together until soft and fluffy. Gradually add the eggs, beating well between additions. Stir in the flour and spices.
5 Stir in the fruit purée, then the almonds and fruits. Spoon into the tin and level the surface. Bake for 2-2 ½ hours, until a skewer comes out clean. Cool in the tin.
6 When cold, remove from the tin and peel away the lining paper. Place on a serving plate. Heat the apricot jam until warm and runny. Brush over the top of the cake, arrange the nuts, then brush over any remaining apricot glaze.
© British Lion Eggs, www.eggrecipes.co.uk

29 Monday

30 Tuesday

31 Wednesday

1 Thursday

2 Friday

3 Saturday

4 Sunday

Every picture tells a story

Nannie was our rock

My nannie was a dinner lady and here she is at Brotherton School making her last Christmas pudding, the day before she retired. She was born in 1901, one of a family of nine children, and became a single parent when she was 19.

When I was growing up, nannie was our rock, especially after my father died when I was aged 12. She had many talents – cooking, knitting, crochet and sewing.

I was never short of beautiful dresses and cardigans. She was a member of the Women's Institute as well as being on the committee of the local Darby and Joan club.

After I had my own children, she would often visit and help me if I was stuck with something. She taught me that it is possible to do anything you want to; never give up, keep trying until you succeed. To the end of her life, nannie had lovely brown hair which I hoped to inherit, but sadly did not.

Pamela Piper, via email

On this week...

December 29, 1975 – End to battle of the sexes
New laws introducing women's right to equal pay came into force on this day. The Sex Discrimination and Equal Pay Acts made it illegal for women to be paid less than their male colleagues. Employers were no longer allowed to advertise specifically for males or female, and new terms, such as 'fire fighters' were to be introduced instead of 'firemen'.

Home hints

Pack away your Christmas lights neatly by winding them around an old hosepipe wheel. Next year you'll be thankful when your lights are tangle-free and ready to get you into the festive spirit again!

Wise words

"You don't need to BE the best, you just need to DO your best"

I was never very good at sports at school and after one particularly fretful sports day my dad said these wise words – which have stuck with me ever since.

Linda Berry, Wolverhampton

Headgear of yesteryear

This is a photo of my great-granddad when he was serving in the Great War. He was married in 1914, so would have gone into service not long afterwards. He was in the Royal Horse Artillery. I don't know much about his time in the war, but I do know he served in Mesopotamia for part of it. He looks so smart, and so young, in this photograph.

Caroline Marsden, via email

Recipe of the week

Crispy Lamb Canapés with Seville Orange Cream

Serves: 6
Preparation time: 15 minutes
Cooking time: 3 minutes

50ml (2fl.oz) soured cream or thick plain natural yoghurt
1tbsp Seville orange marmalade
2 slices rye bread, cut into 20 small squares
100g (3 1/2oz) cooked roast lamb, shredded
2 spring onions, finely shredded and chilled in ice cold water
Pinch ground cayenne or chilli pepper, to garnish

1 In a small bowl, mix together the cream or yoghurt and marmalade.
2 Place the bread squares on a large serving platter and top each square with a spoonful of the cream mixture.
3 If using previously roasted lamb, heat a large non-stick pan and dry fry for 2-3 minutes until hot, cool for 2-3 minutes then arrange over the cream mixture. Garnish with spring onions and cayenne pepper.

Top tip: Starting from scratch? Season and grill 1-2 small leg steaks for 12-16 minutes under a moderate heat, cool for 2-3 minutes, shred with a sharp knife and use as required.
© Simply Beef and Lamb, www.simplybeefandlamb.co.uk

2013 Year-to-view calendar

January

January						
M		7	14	21	28	
Tu	1	8	15	22	29	
W	2	9	16	23	30	
Th	3	10	17	24	31	
F	4	11	18	25		
Sa	5	12	19	26		
Su	6	13	20	27		

February

February						
M		4	11	18	25	
Tu		5	12	19	26	
W		6	13	20	27	
Th		7	14	21	28	
F	1	8	15	22		
Sa	2	9	16	23		
Su	3	10	17	24		

March

March						
M		4	11	18	25	
Tu		5	12	19	26	
W		6	13	20	27	
Th		7	14	21	28	
F	1	8	15	22	29	
Sa	2	9	16	23	30	
Su	3	10	17	24	31	

April

April						
M	1	8	15	22	29	
Tu	2	9	16	23	30	
W	3	10	17	24		
Th	4	11	18	25		
F	5	12	19	26		
Sa	6	13	20	27		
Su	7	14	21	28		

May

May						
M		6	13	20	27	
Tu		7	14	21	28	
W	1	8	15	22	29	
Th	2	9	16	23	30	
F	3	10	17	24	31	
Sa	4	11	18	25		
Su	5	12	19	26		

June

June						
M		3	10	17	24	
Tu		4	11	18	25	
W		5	12	19	26	
Th		6	13	20	27	
F		7	14	21	28	
Sa	1	8	15	22	29	
Su	2	9	16	23	30	

July

July						
M	1	8	15	22	29	
Tu	2	9	16	23	30	
W	3	10	17	24	31	
Th	4	11	18	25		
F	5	12	19	26		
Sa	6	13	20	27		
Su	7	14	21	28		

August

August						
M		5	12	19	26	
Tu		6	13	20	27	
W		7	14	21	28	
Th	1	8	15	22	29	
F	2	9	16	23	30	
Sa	3	10	17	24	31	
Su	4	11	18	25		

September

September						
M		2	9	16	23	30
Tu		3	10	17	24	
W		4	11	18	25	
Th		5	12	19	26	
F		6	13	20	27	
Sa		7	14	21	28	
Su	1	8	15	22	29	

October

October						
M		7	14	21	28	
Tu	1	8	15	22	29	
W	2	9	16	23	30	
Th	3	10	17	24	31	
F	4	11	18	25		
Sa	5	12	19	26		
Su	6	13	20	27		

November

November						
M		4	11	18	25	
Tu		5	12	19	26	
W		6	13	20	27	
Th		7	14	21	28	
F	1	8	15	22	29	
Sa	2	9	16	23	30	
Su	3	10	17	24		

December

December						
M		2	9	16	23	30
Tu		3	10	17	24	31
W		4	11	18	25	
Th		5	12	19	26	
F		6	13	20	27	
Sa		7	14	21	28	
Su	1	8	15	22	29	

2015 Year-to-view calendar

January

January						
M		5	12	19	26	
Tu		6	13	20	27	
W		7	14	21	28	
Th	1	8	15	22	29	
F	2	9	16	23	30	
Sa	3	10	17	24	31	
Su	4	11	18	25		

February

February						
M		2	9	16	23	
Tu		3	10	17	24	
W		4	11	18	25	
Th		5	12	19	26	
F		6	13	20	27	
Sa		7	14	21	28	
Su	1	8	15	22		

March

March						
M		2	9	16	23	30
Tu		3	10	17	24	31
W		4	11	18	25	
Th		5	12	19	26	
F		6	13	20	27	
Sa		7	14	21	28	
Su	1	8	15	22	29	

April

April						
M		6	13	20	27	
Tu		7	14	21	28	
W	1	8	15	22	29	
Th	2	9	16	23	30	
F	3	10	17	24		
Sa	4	11	18	25		
Su	5	12	19	26		

May

May						
M		4	11	18	25	
Tu		5	12	19	26	
W		6	13	20	27	
Th		7	14	21	28	
F	1	8	15	22	29	
Sa	2	9	16	23	30	
Su	3	10	17	24	31	

June

June						
M	1	8	15	22	29	
Tu	2	9	16	23	30	
W	3	10	17	24		
Th	4	11	18	25		
F	5	12	19	26		
Sa	6	13	20	27		
Su	7	14	21	28		

July

July						
M		6	13	20	27	
Tu		7	14	21	28	
W	1	8	15	22	29	
Th	2	9	16	23	30	
F	3	10	17	24	31	
Sa	4	11	18	25		
Su	5	12	19	26		

August

August						
M		3	10	17	24	31
Tu		4	11	18	25	
W		5	12	19	26	
Th		6	13	20	27	
F		7	14	21	28	
Sa	1	8	15	22	29	
Su	2	9	16	23	30	

September

September						
M		7	14	21	28	
Tu	1	8	15	22	29	
W	2	9	16	23	30	
Th	3	10	17	24		
F	4	11	18	25		
Sa	5	12	19	26		
Su	6	13	20	27		

October

October						
M		5	12	19	26	
Tu		6	13	20	27	
W		7	14	21	28	
Th	1	8	15	22	29	
F	2	9	16	23	30	
Sa	3	10	17	24	31	
Su	4	11	18	25		

November

November						
M		2	9	16	23	30
Tu		3	10	17	24	
W		4	11	18	25	
Th		5	12	19	26	
F		6	13	20	27	
Sa		7	14	21	28	
Su	1	8	15	22	29	

December

December						
M		7	14	21	28	
Tu	1	8	15	22	29	
W	2	9	16	23	30	
Th	3	10	17	24	31	
F	4	11	18	25		
Sa	5	12	19	26		
Su	6	13	20	27		

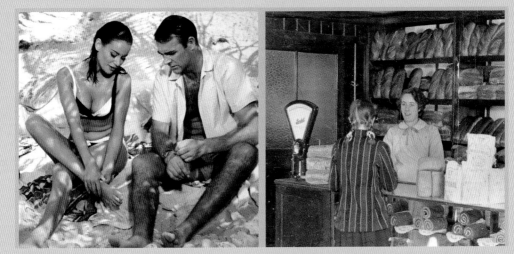

RELAX & UNWIND

Only window dressing!

BY: TREVOR BENTLY

It's a new year and Margaret discovers a new skill

It was a dull winter Monday and Margaret was on her way to work, her breath billowing in the cold air. As she walked along the frosty pavements, she thought of her day ahead in the charity shop where she was a volunteer.

It would begin with opening the bulging bags of donated clothes and bric-a-brac and separating them into three piles. Stuff that was beyond repair, clothes that would be saleable if washed and mended and then all the items that only needed pricing before going on sale.

In the afternoon, she would be behind the till (a task reserved for more experienced volunteers) and would be able to chat to the customers. That was half the battle, Margaret thought, being pleasant to the people who came in to the shop to encourage them to make a purchase and come again.

Since retiring from her office job, she had come to enjoy her voluntary work – the only fly in the ointment was Claire, the new manager. Claire was determined to change the shop's image and increase sales. She made it clear that she regarded the volunteers as fuddy-duddies if they questioned her innovations – such as the window-dressing. Margaret cringed every time the display was revamped.

Averting her eyes from the unseasonal selection of strapless cocktail dresses oddly teamed with riding boots, Margaret entered the shop.

"We're in for a quiet day today," her fellow volunteer, Rosemary, grinned. "The boss is away!"

"Claire is off?"

"Phoned to say she didn't want to spread her germs around – she's got a bad cold."

Well, that was a point in Claire's favour; Margaret had no time for martyrs who struggled in with streaming colds. She reminded herself of her New Year's resolution to focus on the good points of people she found difficult to love – and Claire was definitely in that category.

Margaret had no time for martyrs

Soon she was enjoying herself in Rosemary's easy company. Customers drifted in with various requests: 'Any romance paperbacks?' or 'Got a warm coat in a size 18?'. Most were content to browse through the racks of clothes or the shelves of books and DVDs.

While Rosemary was in the back room having a cup of tea, Margaret wondered to herself if there was any way she could take advantage of Claire's absence. After all, when the cat's away… A cheeky grin crossed her face as she had a flash of inspiration. Selecting a few items from the womenswear section, she made her way to the window at the front of the store.

Working swiftly, she supplemented the mannequins' eveningwear with thick knitted cardigans and long woollen scarves. She found a beret for the head of one model and, as a finishing touch, slipped a pair of bright red mittens on the most elegant one.

'There, that's a bit more seasonal', she thought stepping back to admire her efforts. 'Sucks to Claire. Bare shoulders in January, indeed!'.

Rosemary saw the joke and they chuckled merrily together through the afternoon. Several customers commented on the striking window display that had drawn them in to search for seasonal outfits. When it was time for Margaret to go home, she took off her tabard and hung it on its hook in the musty-smelling back room, still smiling at her own daring.

Through the week, she added more props to her display. An open umbrella protected one model from the elements and a pair of fleecy lined boots enhanced the wintry theme.

"That's become your pet project," Rosemary commented. "It has really perked you up."

On Thursday, the phone rang in the back room and Rosemary answered it. She said: "That was Claire. She's over the worst, she says, so she'll be back tomorrow. Do you think we should put the window back to the way it was? It seems a shame to dismantle all your hard work."

"No, we might as well leave it as it is," Margaret

ILLUSTRATION: KATE DAVIES

"Claire can always change it again..."

replied boldly. "Claire can always change it again, if she wants to."

On Friday morning, Margaret stepped forth a little more reluctantly than usual. She had relished the 'holiday' atmosphere in the shop while the manager was away, but she reflected that, maybe, it was just as well that things would now return to normal.

As she pushed open the shop door, she was startled to find herself engulfed in a big hug. Throwing her arms around Margaret, Claire exclaimed: "Well done, you!" She was clutching a copy of the local paper in one hand. "Look,

Margaret! We've won a prize in the Gazette's Deck Your Windows competition."

After Margaret had replaced her coat with her tabard, Claire spread the paper on the counter and read out: "Manager Claire Todd has created a splendid mixture of fun and fashion at St Martin's Hospice charity shop and scooped our voluntary sector prize."

For once, Margaret was lost for words. She gazed at her jauntily dressed mannequins in the photographs of the winning displays and wondered if it was wrong of her to feel distinctly miffed at Claire for taking all the credit. Then, remembering her New Year's resolution, she accepted a plastic beaker of bubbly and raised it with a smile: "Here's to us!"

After all, January was traditionally a time for fresh starts, wasn't it?

Quick quiz

How many of these general knowledge questions can you answer? Turn the page upside down to see if you're right

1 Who said: "Give a girl the right shoes and she can conquer the world"?

2 From the Agatha Christie books, what is Miss Marple's first name?

3 By which name is director Allen Stewart Konigsberg better known?

4 What does the acronym AKA stand for?

5 Which fictional detective was known for saying: "Book 'em, Danno" ?

6 Which actress is 'A Rude Lass Runs' when the letters of her name are rearranged?

7 How much is the letter J worth in a game of Scrabble

8 Who was the first actor to play Dr Who?

9 Who sang the theme to the Bond film Thunderball?

10 Which British snooker player was given the nickname 'The Whirlwind'?

11 What is Retsina?

12 In America this fragrant herb is called 'cilantro', but what do we call it in the UK?

13 What was Paddington Bear's favourite food?

14 How many signs of the zodiac are there?

15 Who was the voice of the genie in Disney's Aladdin?

16 What were the names of the Famous Five?

17 What colour is the circle on the Japanese flag?

18 Which planet is the second biggest in our solar system?

19 How many spots are there in total on the faces of two dice?

20 What is measured using the 'Scoville' scale?

1 Marilyn Monroe, 2 Jane, 3 Woody Allen, 4 Also Known As, 5 Steve McGarrett, Hawaii Five-O, 6 Ursula Andress, 7 Eight, 8 William Hartnell, 9 Tom Jones, 10 Jimmy White, 11 Greek wine, 12 Coriander, 13 Marmalade sandwiches, 14 Twelve, 15 Robin Williams, 16 George, Anne, Dick, Julian and Timmy, 17 Red, 18 Saturn, 19 Forty-two, 20 The spiciness of chilli peppers

Let's go down the high street

Our daily bread

When only a few homes had the luxury of a fridge – let alone a freezer – food shopping had to be done on a daily basis. Although the first self-service Sainsbury's opened in Croydon in 1950, the concept of a one-stop shop was slow to take off and most of us continued to buy bread from the baker, meat from the butcher and our fruit and vegetables from the greengrocer. Some of these were well-known names such as Dewhurst, Home & Colonial and Mac Fisheries with branches throughout the country, but most local shops were family-run businesses.

The butcher's (or 'meat purveyors' as some rather grandly styled themselves) was invariably chilly, with sawdust strewn over the floor and a separate cashier who handled the money. For those on a tight budget, the butcher's homemade faggots were a tasty weekday option, but everybody stretched their pennies to have a proper roast joint for dinner on Sunday.

Most of what was on sale in the greengrocer's was seasonal, locally grown produce although there were a few exotic goods, such as bananas, on offer as well, if you were lucky. Unlike today, when we can select our own items and bag them, customers were discouraged from handling the goods which meant that the odd bruised apple or squashed tomato quite often found its way into the bottom of the bag!

The baker's smelled invitingly of freshly baked bread and this was where you could buy regional delicacies such as lardy cakes in Gloucestershire or curd tarts in Yorkshire, all made on the premises. As for special

A trip to the baker's for an iced-finger bun was a real treat. And the smell of fresh baked bread, as you walked through the door, was simply heavenly!

occasions – that meant cream cakes for tea!

The next port of call was the grocer's shop where butter, in the shape of a barrel, was displayed on the counter. Chunks were cut off to order and wrapped in greaseproof paper. Whole cheeses were expertly sliced with a wire. Tinned goods included Smedley's fruit and soups from Crosse & Blackwell. Broken biscuits were a popular bargain.

There was no need to lug heavy shopping back home as most shops offered a delivery service. Or you could put your purchases in a basket on wheels. All that changed in the Seventies with the arrival of the ubiquitous plastic carrier bags that we now struggle to avoid using!

"I volunteered for

After Catherine Davies inadvertently joined the Wrens she threw herself into every opportunity

In February 1967 I was off sick from my job as a telephonist at the Royal Hotel, Bristol, with tonsillitis. My GP told me to stay off work, resting my throat for two weeks. A week later, I was feeling fine, and my friend Sue asked me to go into Bristol with her. She was back home, in her smart new Wrens uniform, on her first leave from Dauntless. We went shopping in the city, but first Sue had some papers to drop off at the recruiting office in the centre of the city. While we were there talking to the recruiting officer, a male commander came in. "Great shot," he said, "a recruiting officer, new recruit in uniform and her friend asking about joining too!" I assured him I had no intention of joining anything requiring a uniform thank you very much! But he came back with his camera and told me it would just be for a photo in the Navy News, so I agreed. He asked my name and we left for our shopping trip.

Imagine my horror to see the photo, and the caption, 'Miss Cathy Higgins, interested in joining the Wrens too', on the front page of the Bristol Evening Post a couple of days later! When I got back to work my boss said it had been very difficult for the hotel in my absence and asked me to train one of the receptionists on the switchboard. Naively I did, then they handed me my cards and a week's pay in lieu of notice, as I was obviously not going to tell them I had applied to join the

Catherine (front row, second left) strikes a traditional pose with her colleagues

Navy during my paid sick leave!

My father was furious and had a very animated phone call with the recruiting office! Eventually, the office said that I was welcome to try for the WRNS. I half-heartedly went along, went through the application process and was enlisted as a Radio Operator and went to Dauntless for my initial training.

While I was training, our group were asked to represent the WRNS at the ceremony in Trafalgar Square when a bust of the Second World War First Sea Lord, Admiral Cunningham, was unveiled by Prince Philip, Duke of Edinburgh. The idea was that we had plenty of time to train in marching up and down steps that curved from narrow to broad. We had our weekend leave immediately before going up to London and I proudly took my uniform home to

show my family. Unfortunately, while out for the evening with some friends I left my uniform in a boy's car. When I got back to Dauntless and realised my mistake I was allowed to phone my long-suffering Dad, who went to the boy's home and drove through the night to Burghfield, leaving my bag with one of the cooks at 5am!

After training, I was stationed at Soberton Towers near Petersfield but, due to suffering problems with migraines, I was given a medical change of trade to Wren Air Mechanic. This meant another stint at Dauntless, then off to Arbroath in Scotland for my training on the out-of-service aircraft there. There were just two girls and around 14 lads on our course. Mary came top and I came second – well, we had to show the men that we could beat them at what they regarded as a male domain!

After this I was posted to

everything!"

Catherine didn't follow her dad's advice and volunteered for everything

the 'Visting Aircraft' section at RNAS Yeovilton, HMS Heron, in Somerset. I really enjoyed my time there, and qualified to work on all sorts of aircraft, from the Red Arrows' Gnat to the USA's huge MAC Globemaster. Among visitors I welcomed Petula Clark, who was filming Goodbye Mr Chips, and a certain Lt. Charles Windsor, who flew in as a student pilot.

My dad had always said 'never volunteer', so, of course, I volunteered for anything going! They were looking for a Wren to spend the summer weekends of 1968 flying in the Whirlwind SAR helicopter

on demonstrations at various country shows and air days. The crew would place me in an inflatable dingy on the grass and then fly away. I would fire off a flare and the helicopter would return to 'rescue' me. Great fun!

I also joined the canoe club, who had a model Phantom built. We started to go to water carnivals with the Phantom mounted on a canoe and towed by the lads, me perched on top in shorts and a top with a banner saying 'Miss Fly Navy' on it! We won several carnivals that year, and one of the highlights of my time in the Wrens was being asked to open

the Air Day 1969, perched on my Phantom (which was fixed to a trolley usually used for ammo and towed along by a tractor!), waving to the crowds!

In August 1968, we were told that a Dutch squadron of anti-submarine bombers were coming to us for two weeks to take part in a NATO exercise and would be here for that Air Day. We were asked to help further Anglo-Dutch relations and so, after fixing a pilot's oil filter as soon as they arrived, I ended up marrying Sgt Pilot Kees van Zoen in December 1969 and leaving the WRNS to live in Holland for the next 19 years!

Is this goodbye?

BY: DAVID WASS

Grace's husband says it's time to retire from the job she loves

Grace smiled at the sound of a wolf-whistle as she stood up to address everyone assembled in the lounge of Greenways. She guessed the culprit was Major Butterworth.

"All present except for Florence," Brenda, her assistant manager, reported. "She can't find her teeth."

"Right, thanks." Claire scanned the 30 residents seated around the room. They were going to be shocked by her news – almost as shocked as she had been when her husband, Peter, had made the suggestion.

When he'd booked a table at her favourite restaurant, she assumed he would be discussing their forthcoming wedding anniversary. Instead he said: "I've done the sums and I think we can afford for you to retire."

Claire had frozen, her wine glass halfway to her lips. "But I'm only just 60!"

Peter urged: "Think about it. No more setting the alarm for six every morning. And we could go off on holiday at a moment's notice."

"But how would I spend my time?"

He clicked his tongue. "Have you noticed the state of the garden? Those red roses you loved so much are covered in black spot every summer. And you'd have time to cook things like chutneys and jams again."

Grace had to admit that some things had gone by the board in the 20 or so years that she'd been running Greenways Home for the Elderly.

Peter added: "Anyway, when I retired you asked what I was going to do with my time and look at me now – I don't know how I found time to go to work."

She couldn't argue with that. "There will be a lot of sorting out to do."

"I know, but it will be worth it," Peter said cheerfully, picking up his soup spoon.

To her surprise, Grace had quickly received a good offer for the business. Although the contract hadn't

"I don't know how I found time to go to work"

been signed yet, she felt it was only fair to let the residents know that Greenways would soon be under new ownership.

"Is this going to take long?" a voice wavered, "Only my daughter is due here any time now."

Grace looked over to where 90-year-old Phyllis was waving her walking stick like a windscreen wiper. Every day she expected a visit from her daughter who lived abroad and rarely appeared at Greenways.

"Not too long, Phyllis. If Florence isn't here shortly we'll start without her.

"Lost her teeth again, has she?" the Major boomed. "It'll be a long wait then." Grace watched him march slowly towards the double doors, his back surprisingly straight for a man whose leg had been damaged by a bullet in the war.

"She who's lost shouldn't hesitate," a lady in a pink cardigan called out. "You should have grabbed the horns as soon as you came in."

"Thank you, Rita," Grace called back. "Just a little more patience, please."

Rita always made her smile. She had a wealth of favourite sayings, even if they were a little mixed up.

A woman wearing furry green slippers said: "If you're going to talk about the gravy, last night's was like coloured water. Someone needs to tell the cook that veg can't swim."

In a former life, Marjorie had presented a cookery programme on TV and the menu rarely met with her approval.

"No, Marjorie, I'm not. Since you mention it, though, Brenda will have a word with the chef."

A male nurse pointed at the doorway and Grace added: "Ah, here comes Florence. She must have found her teeth."

A stout figure hobbled in, closely followed by the Major. "Found 'em in one of her shoes," he said triumphantly. "Process of elimination."

"I was the one that found them," Florence snapped.

"Don't bite the hand that finds," Rita put in.

"Can we get on?" Phyllis asked. "I don't want to

Grace swallowed a lump in her throat

miss my daughter."

Grace clapped her hands. "If you will all settle down I'll tell you why we're here."

"I bet it's about the minibus," said a man in dark glasses. "The tyres were let down after our trip to the zoo."

"The zoo, eh?" said a lady in a woolly blue hat, brandishing her knitting needle at him. "I always wondered where you came from!"

Someone sniggered and soon peals of laughter echoed round the room. Trying to keep a straight face, Grace said: "If you don't mind, I'd like to get on."

The room was hushed.

"This week we reached a landmark. Greenways has been serving people like your good selves for 21 years."

"It's a celebration!" the Major roared, applauding. "Come on, you ungrateful shower, put your hands together for the boss."

Everyone clapped and cheered.

Grace swallowed a lump in her throat and tried to focus on her notes. She was about to continue when a silvery soprano floated across the room, "21 today, 21 today…"

Rose had been a professional opera singer. Grace felt tears welling up in her eyes as, one by one, everyone joined in. When they eventually fell silent, she heard herself saying: "Thank you. All I can add to that lovely sentiment is that I'm looking forward to the next 21 years."

Pulling a tissue from her pocket, she hurried from the room. Peter would just have to wait a little longer for his homemade chutney and perfect roses – Greenways needed her more.

Quick quiz

How many of these general knowledge questions can you answer? Turn the page upside down to see if you're right

1 Who said: "Nothing is impossible, the word itself says 'I'm possible!' "?

2 In the novel Pride and Prejudice, what is Mr Darcy's first name?

3 By which name was actor Ermes Effron Borgnino better known?

4 In banking, what does the acronym PIN stand for?

5 Which cartoon character has the catchphrase 'Doh!' ?

6 Which famous dancer is 'I Tread Safer' when the letters of his name are rearranged?

7 In chess which piece can only move diagonally?

8 Which actress has appeared both as Alf Garnett's daughter in Till Death Us Do Part and more recently as Mrs Hudson in Sherlock?

9 The song Raindrops Keep Fallin' On My Head won an Oscar in 1969, but which film was it from?

10 Which World Darts Champion was given the nickname 'The Power'?

11 What is the literal meaning of Crème Brulee?

12 What are 'porcini' a type of?

13 Originating in colonial India, what is the breakfast dish of hard-boiled eggs, rice and fish called?

14 Which astrological sign is represented by a ram?

15 Which American actor provided the voice for 'Sully' in the film Monsters Inc?

16 From the Harry Potter books, can you name all the Weasley children?

17 There are three colours on the Irish flag, what are they and in which order do they appear?

18 Titan is the name of a moon orbiting which planet in our solar system?

PIC REX FEATURES

1 Audrey Hepburn, 2 Fitzwilliam, 3 Ernest Borgnine, 4 Personal Identification Number, 5 Homer Simpson, 6 Fred Astaire, 7 Bishop, 8 Una Stubbs, 9 Butch Cassidy and The Sundance Kid, 10 Phil Taylor, 11 Burnt Cream, 12 Mushroom, 13 Kedgeree, 14 Aries, 15 John Goodman, 16 Bill, Charlie, Percy, Fred, George, Ron, Ginny, 17 Green, white, orange, 18 Saturn

Let's go down the high street

Time for a cuppa

Where better to discuss the latest gossip than over a light lunch at The Copper Kettle?

The high street offered numerous places in which to take a rest from shopping and to meet friends for a chat. Long before the advent of Starbucks and Costa, there was a coffee bar in most towns. Here youngsters met to sit round formica-topped tables, drinking frothy coffee out of pyrex cups. Older customers were usually driven out by the noise of the hit parade being played loudly on the juke box. The Kardomah coffee bar in Swansea was famously the haunt of the young Dylan Thomas and his mates – known locally as 'the Kardomah boys'.

Tea rooms (invariably called The Copper Kettle or The Cosy Nook) provided a quieter refuge for shoppers who wanted a nice cuppa with a scone or a toasted tea cake. Fuller's tea rooms are still fondly remembered for their delicious walnut cake topped with fondant icing. At the other end of the scale, Londoners enjoyed eating in vast Lyons Corner Houses where they were serenaded by an orchestra while being served afternoon tea by waitresses known as nippies.

There were no waitresses at the ABC (Aerated Bread Company) tea rooms which were pioneers of self-service. George Bernard Shaw was a fan of ABCs – they earn several mentions in his diaries – and so, apparently, was Agatha Christie. In her novel, The Secret Adversary, the hero goes into an ABC shop and orders 'eggs and bacon and coffee'.

Practically every high street had a hotel that had once been a coaching inn and the lounge bar provided a meeting place for anyone who fancied a pre-lunch pint (for the men) or a schooner of cream sherry (for the ladies). Children were not admitted, of course, but their idea of heaven was more likely to be a banana split or a knickerbocker glory at the nearest milk bar.

For a nice meal out, where better than the nearest Berni Inn? In the comfort of a mock-Tudor dining room you could enjoy a typical menu starting with a melon boat (garnished with a maraschino cherry), followed by a steak or plaice with chips and peas, rounded off by a Black Forest gateau or a selection from the cheese board, all washed down with an Irish coffee.

"My sunshine days"

Lessons on the beach were just part of Christine Bagg's idyllic Cyprus childhood

My schooldays, 54 years ago, were very different from that of my grandson, Alex's, nowadays. I call them my 'Sunshine Days', as I spent much of my childhood in sunny Cyprus, where my father was serving as part of a peacekeeping force.

In those days, wives and families were allowed to accompany soldiers, but the available accommodation varied hugely. My father, who had gone on ahead of us to his posting in Famagusta, had found a little house to rent. In some towns the families lived within the barracks compound, but in Famagusta we lived out in the local community.

That first house failed to meet mum's critical standards. After close inspection of its dark corners and suspect plumbing she declared it 'simply wouldn't do'. She was right; despite endless spraying to keep the cockroaches at bay, they soon reappeared. So we moved to a flat, sharing a communal courtyard with some other service families where we children played together under the vines. One side of the courtyard backed on to a dark, mysterious orange grove and when we felt very daring we would climb through the wire fence to explore. We must have lived in that flat almost a year because I can remember grapes changing from small seeds to huge juicy black bunches, ripening where they hung outside our windows.

I am not sure why we moved again. Perhaps, mum missed having her own garden. In any event, our next house had Greek Cypriot neighbours one side and Turkish Cypriots the other. In those days, before the island was partitioned, the two communities lived alongside each other, sometimes in harmony, sometimes not. Mum soon got tired of rushing out to rescue her children or washing from the garden whenever the neighbours started throwing stones across

There was always plenty of fun to be had in the sunshine and learning to swim was a huge achievement

it at each other, so we moved to our final home on the island, a bungalow in a street where other service families lived. I think that was my favourite home because once again there were children from my school to play with.

Despite the moves I always went to the same army school. A local coach would arrive each morning at 7.30am to pick us up ready for lessons starting at 8am. We all carried a round, brightly coloured plastic water bottle on a strap across our chests. It was drummed into us that we should never go out without a full bottle of water. In summer the danger of sunstroke was very real so we were encouraged to keep in the shade and drink regularly.

An armed soldier always accompanied us on the coach. One day there was a shooting incident somewhere on the island causing general panic and unrest and the coaches failed to appear, so the army organised troop transport lorries to take us home. That was very exciting.

School ended at 1pm before the heat peaked, and then we were driven home in time for a light lunch followed by an afternoon nap. After that it was outside to play or down to the beach to swim. To make up for the short day we had school on Saturdays as well. In the summer the lessons would be taken on the beach, then all the mums and dads would arrive for an afternoon of family swimming and dozing under umbrellas.

I remember that out in the bay was a raft constructed from logs. The men would swim out to the raft then dive off it. How I wanted to go out to it too, but I was still using a rubber ring. It was a huge incentive to learn to swim properly and ditch the rubber ring. When the day came that dad declared I was now big enough to swim out to the raft with him I felt very grown up indeed. Sadly, once I reached it, the raft was a bit of a disappointment as there was nothing to do other than dive from it. I don't know what I was expecting, but I was quickly bored and asked dad to swim with me back to the shore. But at least I learned to swim properly!

We were all sorry when the time came to return to England. Despite the difficulties, such as periods when the water was suddenly turned off, the air of danger when hostilities were sparked off in the community, and the men's curfew which meant we always had to be home by the evening, we all loved it there.

A game of let's pretend

BY: KEITH HAVERS

Peter still knows how to brighten a small boy's day

From the back seat of the car Matthew whined: "But I want to play with Simon today. He's my best friend."

"You have all of half-term to play with Simon," replied Matthew's mum. "And you don't see nan and granddad very often."

The six year old sulked all the way down the motorway. When they arrived, the big fuss his grandmother made of him did nothing to improve his mood.

"How about going out in the garden?" suggested Peter, his granddad. "Let the women have a natter on their own."

Peter had left a football in the middle of the lawn but Matthew showed little interest in playing with it. Picking up a cane from a pile near the shed, Peter playfully poked Matthew in the back. This brought the first hint of a smile to the lad's face.

"How about a sword fight?"

Peter selected another cane and handed it over. Matthew gripped it, ready to do battle.

"Wait a minute," Peter said. "We have to insult each other first."

The boy gave him a puzzled look.

"You know. Call each other names."

"Why?"

"Why else would we be fighting?"

Peter pointed his stick at his grandson. "You, sir, are a blackguard and a varlet! I shall slice off your ears and turn out your gizzards!"

"What's a blag… blag – that thing you said?"

"Never mind. It's just a nasty name. Now you say, 'You are a knave and I shall run you through with my trusty sword'."

"You are a knave and I'll run after you with my rusty sword."

"Trusty swor… oh, never mind."

Peter angled his cane and they crossed sticks. "En garde!"

Their canes clattered together in a frenzy of swordplay. Matthew giggled uncontrollably as he

"What's a blag…blag – that thing you said?"

thrust and parried with his stick. The pair fought up and down the lawn until Peter decided it was time to bring things to a conclusion. Holding his weapon to one side, he indicated Matthew to drive his cane under his armpit.

Peter gripped it between his arm and ribs and fell to the ground in mock agony. "Ah!" he cried. "You have done for me!"

"I won! I won!" shouted Matthew.

"You are the victor and I lie here, dying. Only the kiss of a fair maiden can save me."

Matthew stood over him, confused by these words.

"Go on!" hissed Peter. "Go in and tell your nan that only the soft lips of a fair maid can resurrect me."

Propped up on one elbow, he watched the boy race back in through the patio door.

"Nan! Nan! You have to come quick. Granddad needs a kiss or he can't get up."

"Matthew!" his mum said. "What have I told you about interrupting grown-ups when they are talking? And did you wipe your feet?"

"But mum," Matthew wailed, "Granddad's on the ground and he can't get up!"

The women exchanged a glance. With a worried frown, his grandmother hurried outside, followed by her daughter and Matthew.

"Whatever's wrong?" she cried.

"Ah," smiled Peter, "the fairest maid in the land has come to my aid."

"Get up off that damp grass, you silly old devil," she scolded. "You'll catch pneumonia."

"Only the gentle touch of your sweet lips will bring me to my feet," Peter insisted.

Matthew giggled. His granddad knew how to put on a fine act. Realising that her husband wasn't going to abandon his game, nan knelt down and gave him a swift peck on the forehead.

"Is that it?" he asked. "It must be on the lips or I fear I shall not recover."

Sighing, she stooped over him once more and kissed him full on the mouth. Peter wrapped his arms around his wife to pull her closer and as she struggled to free herself, they both rolled over on the grass.

"Now I've got grass stains on my trousers"

"You clumsy old fool!" she shouted as she got to her feet. "Now I've got grass stains on my cream trousers."

Her cross words were drowned out by the laughter of her daughter and grandson. Matthew hopped from one foot to the other at the sight of his grandparents tumbling around on the lawn. He hadn't realised old people could be so much fun.

"Oh come on, Nell. You have to see the funny side," Peter pleaded.

Matthew's nan couldn't be angry any longer. She helped her husband to his feet and brushed him down before they all went in to have tea.

On their way home in the car, Matthew's mother said: "If you like, you can have half an hour playing with Simon, if his mum says that's okay."

In the rear-view mirror, she saw him shrug.

"A few hours ago you were complaining that you'd rather spend time with your best friend than visit your nan and granddad."

"I've decided Simon isn't my best friend any more," Matthew announced.

His mum glanced in the mirror. "Oh?"

"He's still my friend, but now he's my second-best friend. Granddad's my best friend. He makes up awesome games."

"Well, that's true."

"And he's funny."

His mother smiled. She had almost forgotten how amusing her dad could be. When she was growing up she had loved his zest for life and sense of fun. Her son's words reminded her that he had always been her best friend, too.

Quick quiz

How many of these general knowledge questions can you answer? Turn the page upside down to see if you're right

PIC: REX FEATURES

1 Who said: "Be yourself, everyone else is taken"?

2 In the novel Great Expectations what is Pip's full name?

3 By which name is actress and singer Doris Mary Ann Kappelhoff better known?

4 What does the acronym ISBN stand for?

5 On a TV game show who utters the catchphrase, 'Deal or no deal?'

6 Which acclaimed guitarist is 'Narcoleptic' when the letters of his name are rearranged?

7 In Monopoly how much do you get from the bank when you pass Go?

PIC: REX FEATURES

8 Which actor played Granddad in Only Fools and Horses?

9 Who wrote the songs for the Disney film The Lion King?

10 Which Australian golfer was given the nickname 'The Great White Shark'?

11 What is Farfelle?

12 In America this vegetable is called 'zucchini' but what is it more commonly called in the UK?

13 Which vegetable is the main ingredient in the Russian soup Borscht?

14 Which star sign would you be if you were born on May 1?

15 What type of fish was Nemo in the animated film Finding Nemo?

16 Can you name the children featured in The Lion, The Witch and The Wardrobe?

17 Which three colours feature on the German flag?

18 Which body in our solar system is known as 'the Red Planet'?

19 What is the square root of 576?

20 What is measured on the 'Richter' scale?

1 Oscar Wilde, 2 Philip Pirrip, 3 Doris Day, 4 International Standard Book Number, 5 Noel Edmonds, 6 Eric Clapton, 7 £200, 8 Leonard Pearce, 9 Elton John and Tim Rice, 10 Greg Norman, 11 Butterfly or bow shaped pasta, 12 Courgette, 13 Beetroot, 14 Taurus, 15 Clown Fish, 16 Peter, Edmund, Susan and Lucy Pevensie, 17 Black, red and yellow, 18 Mars, 19 24, 20 The magnitude of an earthquake

Let's go down the high street

Those prams were made for walking... certainly no room in the shops for them

PIC GETTY

Something for everyone

Once the food shopping was done, the high street had a whole range of retail opportunities for all the family. Woolworth sold everything from exercise books with the times tables on the back of their shiny red covers for schoolchildren to packets of Cuthbert's seeds for gardeners. For teenagers, the store's Embassy record label produced cheap cover versions of hit parade numbers while Pick 'n' Mix sweets were a hit with customers of all ages.

Every high street had a sweet shop. Maynard's (famous for their wine gums) had 140 branches across the country offering everything from Palm Toffee with a banana filling to bars of Fry's Five Boys milk chocolate. Children also loved to spend their pocket money in the local toyshop. The boys bought Airfix model aeroplanes to make out of balsa wood or added to their collection of Dinky toys while the girls went for hula hoops or yo-yos – whatever was the latest craze. I-Spy spotters' books appealed to both boys and girls who sent their completed books to Big Chief I-Spy to get an order of merit and a feather.

The grown-ups would be sure to stop by the tobacconist to stock up on their favourite cigarettes – Craven 'A' and Peter Stuyvesant were popular brands but many people smoked Embassy and Kensitas so they could collect the coupons and send away for gifts such as glassware or other household items. The tobacconist also sold pipes and tobacco and Ronson lighters (top of the range were the Wedgwood ones to place next to the box of cigarettes on a side table in the lounge).

For reading matter, shoppers popped into the newsagent for a magazine – Tit-Bits, Picture Post or John Bull – or picked up a copy of the local evening paper from the news vendor bellowing 'Read all abaht it!' on the street corner. If you wanted a book, you could borrow one from the public library or from the Boots lending library which was usually situated to the rear of the chemist shop.

Before heading for home, mum might call in at the wool shop or the haberdasher's if she planned to do some knitting or sewing over the weekend while dad bought whatever he needed for his DIY projects from the ironmonger or a hardware shop.

Dreamboats and

What could tempt Ellie Arlen to 'dump' her Hollywood heartthrob?

We were off to the pictures to see my idol, Roy Rogers! It was an autumn evening in South Yorkshire, 1949. Aged six, I loved that time of year, having Bonfire Night and Christmas to look forward to. With my mum, dad and older sister I was heading for a first showing, around 5pm, at our local cinema, The Grand (a title it never quite lived up to).

Roy Rogers made three films in 1949, seven the year before, so it was a case of 'seen one, seen 'em all'. Nevertheless, 'The King of the Cowboys' was still packing houses at every showing. He plucked us out of our grey post-war days of rationing and making do, into Hollywood's glamorous version of the Old Wild West, where cowboys wore fancy boots and strummed guitars.

Of course, there was a queue, but we didn't mind. Sharing the anticipation upped the excitement. Conversations and friendships were struck up as we shuffled forward.

By the time dad had finally bought our tickets and we stood blinking in the flickering blackness, the usherette's torch couldn't pick out two vacant seats together, let alone four. At least, not in the popular one and nines. Too big to perch on a lap by then, I had to sit on my own among a row of strangers. But those 'strangers' were the locals we'd just queued with outside, so it seemed perfectly safe.

PI: REX FEATURES

A youthful Ellie wanted to be just like her hero Roy Rogers until one fateful trip to the cinema

When Roy rode on to the silver screen in his Stetson hat, astride his famous golden palomino horse called Trigger, and began flirting with his beautiful leading lady (whom we knew to be his real-life wife, Dale Evans) while strumming and singing to his guitar – well, I was right up there with him.

I think all the kids wanted to be like Roy Rogers in those days – even little girls like me. He was so handsome and clean-cut, everything we thought a cowboy hero should be. It felt safe to idolise Roy Rogers. How I yearned to live the dream by running away to America and becoming

a cowgirl. I'd ride the prairie in safety on the back of a wonder horse like Trigger, 'The Smartest Horse in the Movies'.

When the final credits rolled, I was so hooked that I didn't want to be dragged from the adrenalin-charged sweat and cigarette fug of the auditorium, back into the humdrum life of the world outside. I wanted to 'sit it round' – stay in my seat for the second showing and bask again in the exciting, sun-kissed world of Roy Rogers and California. I bet I had a sulky face as I trailed after my family across the foyer,

swing boats

Family entertainment in a Yorkshire mining town was far removed from the romance of life on the prairie

pushed through the big swing doors and braced myself for the reality slap of the chilly dark Yorkshire night…

But lo and behold, magic had happened while we'd been inside! On the plot of waste ground opposite, a travelling fair, closed and silent as we'd queued, had opened up and was in full swing. All the glittery lights were on; steam engines throbbed, gears cranked and gaily painted rides flashed round and round. Across the road drifted pungent smells of hot machinery and baked potatoes and all sorts of other titillating, exotic undertones. It was my first sighting of a fair, and in those drab austerity days, it seemed as though a wonderland of all the colour and thrills, so lacking in our everyday lives, had

sprung up on our very doorstep.

Best of all, nearest the road, was a row of swing boats. The boats soared up above my head, each with colourful motifs along the sides and two striped, padded ropes to pull, like the rope for ringing bells. They were full of laughing couples, pulling on the ropes in turn to swing each other higher and higher – so high I could see the patterns on the undersides. I desperately wanted a go on one. Of course, I was told I was too young, but those glorious swing boats had imprinted themselves on my mind – it wasn't if, but when I'd have a go on one.

"Giddy-up!" I slapped my rump, dragged myself away and headed for home on my imaginary horse, rounding up my family through the lonesome prairie that in

reality was closely-packed streets of miners' terraced houses. But that evening something wasn't right. I couldn't be bothered to gallop any more. Obsession with the fairground had taken over. A new dream world had opened up – one I could actually touch and savour. I couldn't get my mind off those magical swinging boats. Maybe, came the shocking thought, I might not want to run away to join Roy Rogers and be a cowgirl after all. Did they have fairgrounds in California? Or even celebrate Bonfire Night over there?

Before reaching home I'd done the unthinkable: I'd dumped Roy Rogers, America, even Trigger – the whole Hollywood shebang – in favour of fairground razzmatazz in my own home town!

Someone from Mars

BY: SHEILA LILLEY

Lizzie is suspicious of the alien in her garden

Jake came running in to the kitchen: "Grandma! I saw a spaceman in the garden!"

"That's nice, dear."

Busily shelling peas, Lizzie smiled at her four-year-old grandson's vivid imagination. He was enjoying a holiday with her. With her rosy cheeks and beaming smile, Lizzie seemed to him like a character in a storybook and he called her his Country Grandma.

Jake jumped up and down, his shoes clattering on the stone-flagged floor. "It's true! He's dressed all in white with a helmet on his head."

"Did your spaceman say anything?"

"He said hello and told me not to be scared."

"He speaks good English, then, for someone from Mars."

Jake gave her a pitying look. "He's an earthling, grandma, not an extra-terrible."

"Terrestrial," Lizzie corrected him gently. "Funny that Fergus didn't bark." Dozing by the range, Fergus thumped his tail on hearing his name.

"I don't think Fergus would smell a spaceman through his suit."

Deciding not to get bogged down in technicalities, Lizzie suggested Jake could help her prepare the vegetables. She put some pea pods in front of him and showed him how to snap them open. Jake was fascinated. "That's cool. Mum gets her peas in bags. Do these come from outer space?"

"Certainly not! They're fresh from my garden."

"The spaceman said your vegetables looked nice."

Lizzie began to suspect the spaceman's intentions. The village show, for which she grew prize-winning vegetables, was coming up and there had been cases of sabotage in the past. "So the spaceman fell out of the sky right into my vegetable patch?"

"No, he climbed over the fence."

"Oh, he did, did he? We'll see about that."

Lizzie groped in the cupboard under the sink and pulled out something covered in cobwebs that looked like a baseball bat to Jake.

Lizzie groped in the cupboard under the sink

"It's a copper stick. We used it to wash clothes before washing machines were invented. It might come in handy."

Telling Jake to stay with Fergus in the kitchen, Lizzie crept down the garden path, copper stick held aloft. She could have found her way blindfold, guided by the heady scents of high summer. The bees seemed intoxicated – their heavy droning filled the air. Lizzie respected bees, but also feared them, having been badly stung many years ago. She advanced cautiously.

The perfume of flowers gave way to the musky smell of blackcurrant bushes. At the end of the garden, where a tiny stream murmured, was Lizzie's precious vegetable patch. Using a large bush for cover, Lizzie spied out the land, but saw no one. Then she felt a touch from behind. Spinning round, she was confronted by Jake and Fergus looking up at her.

"Jake, you gave me a turn! I told you to stay in the house. Your spaceman seems to have gone."

"I know. He went over the fence." Jake pointed towards the farmer's meadow.

"Why didn't you tell me?"

"That's what I came to tell you now."

Lizzie relaxed. "Well, I think we've had enough of spacemen for one day. All this isn't getting our lunch ready." She took Jake's hand and they made their way back to the cottage.

Suddenly, Fergus emitted a low growl. Lizzie froze. Ahead of them was something she feared more than spacemen or vegetable saboteurs. A huge ball of hundreds of bees hummed and throbbed. The swarm swung from a branch overhanging the path.

Placing Jake behind her, she whispered: "Turn round ever so slowly and walk back to the stream. Keep very, very quiet."

Thinking it was a game, Jake followed her instructions. As she backed carefully away, the bees paid her no attention. Shaken, she sat down by Jake while she considered what to do next.

They were startled by a cheerful voice. "You've got them settled. That's excellent! Thought I'd lost them for a while."

Fergus jumped up, wagging his tail as a white-

ILLUSTRATION: KATE DAVIES

Something she feared more than spacemen

clad figure clambered over the fence.

"It's the spaceman!" cried Jake.

"It's a beekeeper," corrected Lizzie with a sigh of relief. "Am I glad to see you! I don't know how long we would have been stuck here."

"Best not to go near them," the beekeeper advised. "We'll have to get you across the stream and back indoors round by the meadow."

The voice sounded familiar. Lizzie peered at his face, fuzzy behind the protective mask.

"Jim Wilkins, is that you in there?"

"The very same, Lizzie." Taking Jake's other hand, he helped the little boy jump over the hummocky grass of the meadow. "I've retired

back here. Bought a smallholding. Beekeeping is a profitable sideline."

"You were the boy who told me a bee wouldn't sting if you grasped it firmly," Lizzie reminded him bitterly.

"I got mixed up with stinging nettles. Anyway, you were the girl who promised to wait for me when I went sheep farming in New Zealand."

"You were gone twenty years!"

"Do bees come from outer space?" asked Jake, but no one heard him.

Later, when the bees were safely hived, Jim returned with a jar of honey and a bottle of Champagne. "I was wondering, Lizzie, if we could get to know each other once more…"

Lizzie nodded. "Just so long as you don't go buzzing off to foreign parts ever again."

Jake thought he'd never seen Country Grandma's cheeks so rosy or her smile quite as beaming.

Quick quiz

How many of these general knowledge questions can you answer? Turn the page upside down to see if you're right

1 Who said: "Be the change that you wish to see in the world"?

2 In the novel The Secret Garden, what was Dickon's full name?

3 By what name was actor James Leblanche Stewart better known?

4 In education, what does the acronym GCSE stand for?

5 Which fictional police detective was famous for saying: "Who loves ya, baby?"

6 Which royal is 'Nice Spanners' when the letters of her name are rearranged?

7 When playing Trivial Pursuit how many different colour 'wedges' does a player need to win the game?

8 Which two actors appeared in both Porridge and Open All Hours?

PIC: REX FEATURES

9 Which song, composed by Henri Mancini, won an Academy Award for its appearance in Breakfast at Tiffany's?

10 Which England cricketer was given the nickname 'Fast Freddie'?

11 From which flower is the spice saffron obtained?

12 'Dolmas' is a Turkish dish of lamb and rice wrapped in what?

13 Which nut features in 'Satay' sauce?

14 Which star sign would you be if you were born on March 11?

15 Which American actor provided the voice for Donkey in the Shrek movies?

16 What are the first names of the Bennet sisters in Pride and Prejudice?

17 Which two colours appear on the Polish flag?

18 Which planet is fifth from the sun and the largest in our solar system?

19 How many inches are there in 13 ½ feet?

20 Which gas is most prevalent in the Earth's atmosphere?

Let's go down the high street

The windows to watch

In the Sixties, it became 'trendy' to wear the latest fashion and, for the first time, there was a generation of young men and women who had money to spend on clothes. Boutiques like Chelsea Girl and Richard Shops sprang up to cater for an unprecedented demand for mini skirts, Dolly Rocker dresses, feather boas and white Courrège-style boots – all cheap enough to buy, wear and discard as soon as the next 'in' look came along.

Before that, fashion was aimed solely at adults with the emphasis being on quality and clothes that were intended to last, usually made from natural fabrics. Marks & Spencer could always be relied on for the matching pastel twin sets and sensible pleated skirts that were the wardrobe basics for women of all ages. It was unusual to see women wearing trousers or 'slacks' as they were usually called.

For those on a tighter budget, C & A Modes offered reasonably priced clothes and had a particularly good selection of hats. (However, the C and A didn't stand for Coats and 'Ats as was jokingly claimed but were the initials of the store's German founders, Clemens and August Brenninkmeijer).

For their suits, Van Heusen shirts and ties by Tootal, our menfolk headed to popular gents' outfitters such as Montague Burton (The Tailor of Taste), Hepworth's or John Collier (always remembered as 'the window to watch'). Weekend wear was a sports jacket, a cravat worn with an open-neck shirt and flannel trousers – denim jeans were only worn by cowboys in Westerns.

Children wore miniature versions of grown-up clothes – except that boys wore flannel shorts until they were teenagers when their transition to manhood (and warm knees!) was marked by their first pair of long trousers. When it came to school uniforms, Daniel Neal sold everything from straw boaters to navy knickers in their stores located in London, Bournemouth, Bristol, Cheltenham, Exeter and Birmingham. However, in most cases our mums knitted our regulation navy cardigans and grey knee-length socks to save on the housekeeping money. Ungratefully, we longed for shop-bought ones!

PIC: REX FEATURES

Suits you Sir! Fashionable dressing was not just for the ladies.

Our old country pub

Bitter, bartering, betting and boots were all part of life as a landlord's daughter for Linda Hurdwell

I was almost 15 years old when my parents fulfilled their dream and became tenants of a country pub, The Duke of Edinburgh, not far from Ascot racecourse. It was a rambling, shabby looking building that was draughty and damp and to me, a town girl, it appeared to be in the middle of nowhere. Well, too far from the shops anyway! There were a few cottages and bungalows across the road, and right next door was the saw mill. At the far end of the road was a chicken farm that usually filled the air with all those familiar country smells. The hamlet was surrounded by forest and looked very picturesque.

"Get yerself a cat," were the first words spoken to us by our very first customer, old Ma. She was an enormous woman who could just about squeeze her elderly frame on to one of the public bar chairs as she arrived to have her pint of stout. Often, if she stayed late in the evening, old Ma could be spotted outside with her skirt lifted high. She wasn't always able to make it home to her cottage in time for the call of nature.

Charlie was old Ma's husband and was as skinny as she was large. They never sat together. He would usually stand at the bar, his hands shaking so most of his brown ale landed on the floor before it reached his lips. A blessing the floor was covered in lino in those days. The majority of the regulars were farmhands or builders and would come in after a hard day's work for a quick one, still wearing their mucky Wellington boots, much to my mother's dismay. She yearned to be able to ban boots, but the boots came with the customers that were needed.

Old Harry was another regular and a 'die with his boots on' sort. He was a very suspicious old man, who would grudgingly lay out the exact money for his Guinness. If the beer price increased, it would take Harry a few weeks before he could accept having to pay the extra. It was Harry that gave us the first taste of fresh mushrooms. He would come into the bar with a bag behind his back, full of mushrooms or other such local foods, in exchange for a pint of Guinness of course.

The weekly darts matches

Pub life was never dull for Linda and her parents. The locals enjoyed their drinks and the pub could boast some of the best darts players in the area.

were the highlight of the pub. During the home matches, my mother and I would spend ages making piles of cheese and onion sandwiches for the darting punters. Evidently our pub held some of the best darts players in the area. Ted, the Ascot champion, would carefully aim his dart, wearing a grin that always had a rolled cigarette dangling from it. There would be a deathly hush until double 20 was scored, and then there was much jubilant cheering. Darts matches brought a wonderful community spirit among the folk.

Saturday mornings were another important event. Living near to the Ascot racecourse made the majority of the customers great betting men. Arthur, with his loud laugh, was the 'runner' for the local bookmaker, and would spend Saturday morning on the end of our telephone placing all the bets. Dad would religiously push the old black and white television from our downstairs lounge into the servery of the pub so the punters could whoop or jeer at the televised horse racing.

On Saturday evenings there would often be a grand sing-song, with old Lil playing the ancient bar piano. Tony had a wonderful baritone voice that started everyone off. After a few pints the songs became louder and more raucous, a bar full of song.

Being a publican was hard work in those days. The beer and bitter came in wooden barrels that had to be carefully rolled from the cellar to behind the bar when needed. There was no central heating, which meant the log fires during the winter months had to be swept and topped up with coal or wood to keep the bars cosy.

And, of course, 'last orders gentlemen please' never always actually meant that. People were often very slow to leave, which meant my parents had many a night without enough sleep.

Our kitchen was a cold brick building at the end of the pub that was warmed by the old black boiler and, when sitting quietly, a couple of mice could be seen scampering across the floor, often scared off by my loud screams. We did indeed have to get a cat!

Starry, starry night

BY: HELEN M HUNT

The stars hold precious memories – and a message – for Lucy

Lucy read through her resignation letter one more time, then she printed it out and carefully put it in an envelope. She sighed. The letter was one of the hardest she had ever written.

She took a moment to revel in the peace of the empty office. It wasn't unusual for her to be there alone at that time of night. Her colleagues were all as dedicated as she was, but they had families to go home to.

She had been so absorbed in her task that she hadn't noticed it growing dark outside. Swinging her office chair round, she gazed out of the window. It was a clear autumn night and the sky was full of sparkling stars. She liked to look up at the heavens and marvel at their beauty, so distant in time and space.

When she was a child, her dad had told her about the constellations and he had explained about the various types of stars, all at different stages in their life cycle. He'd told her: "Nebulae are the birthplaces of stars – huge clouds of gas just waiting to burst into life."

One of their conversations had been different from the others, though. The night after they'd been to Lucy's grandmother's funeral he'd said: "See that star up there?"

"Yes," 12-year-old Lucy had breathed, hanging on to his every word.

"That's granny's soul shining down on you from heaven."

Lucy had looked at him with the wide-eyed innocence of childhood: "Really?"

"Yes," he said, brushing away a tear running down his cheek. "So, if you're ever sad about her not being with us any more, you can look up at the night sky and think of her and smile."

"You can look up at the night sky and think of her and smile"

Lucy had never forgotten that. Many years later, she had come home from her father's funeral and thrown open the window to look up at the stars and feel close to him.

That had been ten years ago and since then she had devoted herself to working for this small charity that was searching for a cure for the disease that had taken her wonderful father away from her too soon.

Lucy had always known that she wanted a job that would make a real difference to people's lives. At first she had dreamed of being a doctor but, over the years, had come to realise that her skills were better suited to research. She loved the patterns that numbers made and the excitement when months of work all fell into place.

She'd had countless romantic dinner dates when her companion's eyes had glazed over as she talked about her work. But she didn't care. She knew that what she was doing was valuable. One day the charity's research would result in a medical breakthrough and if they only saved one person's life as a result, it would be worth it.

Every time she looked up at the night sky, she imagined the stars to be the loved ones of all those who had lost someone dear to them. One might be a dear wife, taken from her family before her time; another might be a young soldier who'd died fighting in a far off country. As they lit the darkness with their gentle light, each one sent a message of hope to those left behind.

Lucy returned to reality as she glanced back at the letter from Aston Pharmaceuticals on her desk. The letter offered her a more lucrative job involving less hands-on research than she did with the charity, but better prospects of promotion.

"It's more of a commercial role than you're used to," the suave young director of operations had told her at the interview.

Lucy had nodded and smiled, not wishing to jeopardise her chances, but not too sure about the commercial angle. The increase in salary would be welcome. Money wasn't everything, but it really was about time she moved out of her cramped flat

ILLUSTRATION: KATE DAVIES

Suddenly she knew what she had to do

and into a proper house. Even though the husband and children she had once dreamed of hadn't materialised, she still needed a home of her own.

Moving Aston Pharmaceuticals' letter aside, she picked up the estate agent's details of the pretty cottage that she had viewed over the weekend. If she moved, maybe she could get a cat for company.

She stuck a stamp on the envelope and tucked it in the top of her bag so she wouldn't forget to put it in the letterbox. Posting it seemed more official than putting it in the internal mail. Also, once she'd posted it, she couldn't change her mind and snatch it back in the morning before her boss saw it.

The crisp chill of the evening hit Lucy as she stepped outside. She looked back up at the building,

then turned and walked resolutely away. She gazed at the sky, overwhelmed by the infinite galaxies of stars. All those precious souls, eternally watching over their loved ones.

Suddenly, she knew what she had to do. Cats and cottages could wait; her work here was not finished yet. She tore up the letter and threw it in a bin. Beautiful as the stars were, Lucy didn't want any more souls joining them before their time – not if she could help it.

"Thanks, Dad," she whispered as she strode briskly homeward.

Quick quiz

How many of these general knowledge questions can you answer? Turn the page upside down to see if you're right

PIC REX FEATURES

1 Who said: "You only live once, but if you do it right, once is enough"?

2 Can you name the three musketeers named in Alexandre Dumas' novel?

3 By what name is actress Alicia Christian Foster better known?

4 What does the acronym NIMBY stand for?

5 In science fiction which character frequently said: "Live long and prosper"?

6 Which famous jockey is 'Taken It For Ride' when the letters of his name are rearranged?

7 In Cluedo what is the name of the victim who is inevitably murdered before the game begins?

8 Which actor played Sherlock Holmes on TV from 1984 to 1994?

9 Who is the only person to have sung the theme songs to three Bond films?

10 Which British boxer was given the nickname 'The Hitman'?

11 What is the principle ingredient in Guacamole?

12 In America this vegetable is called 'egg plant' but what is it more commonly called in the UK?

13 What was TV cook Fanny Cradock's husband's name?

14 Which astrological sign is represented by the crab?

15 Who gave voice to Sheriff Woody in the Toy Story films?

16 What were the names of the children in the Addams Family?

17 What is the white shape in the centre of the Somali flag?

18 Can you name the first satellite sent into space?

PIC REX FEATURES

Answers: 1 Mae West, 2 Aramis, Athos, Porthos, 3 Jodie Foster, 4 Not In My Back Yard, 5 Spock, 6 Frankie Dettori, 7 Dr Black, 8 Jeremy Brett, 9 Shirley Bassey, 10 Ricky Hatton, 11 Avocado, 12 Aubergine, 13 Johnny, 14 Cancer, 15 Tom Hanks, 16 Wednesday and Pugsley Addams, 17 Star, 18 Sputnik.

Let's go down the high street

Glamour comes to town

A shampoo and set would set you up for a night out at the Palais with the girls.

A sure sign that the post-war austerity years were over was that women had more time and money to spend on their appearance. Life's little luxuries included fully fashioned Kayser Bondor stockings to go with a pair of stiletto heels from Freeman, Hardy & Willis or Saxone shoe shops.

For beauty products, women went to the chemist, Boots or Timothy Whites & Taylors, where they could buy Palmolive soap 'for a schoolgirl complexion', Pond's vanishing cream or Sunsilk shampoo. Hollywood movies were a big influence and film fans used Max Factor's Pancake foundation to achieve the same flawless complexion as Elizabeth Taylor.

The height of sophistication was a dab of Evening in Paris perfume behind the ears.

Every high street had a ladies' hairdressing establishment in which could be glimpsed a row of women under helmet-shaped driers that looked as though they had just landed from outer space. Salons smelled strongly of perming lotion as everyone wanted curly hair which required a weekly shampoo and set – until Vidal Sassoon changed all that with casual styles that needed nothing more than a cut and blow dry.

Not everyone could afford a weekly visit to the hairdresser so on a Saturday morning it wasn't unusual to see women shopping with their hair in curlers –

covered by a nylon headscarf – ready to be combed out and backcombed later for a night out at the Palais or the Odeon.

Even men were influenced by the stars of Hollywood and 'a Tony Curtis' was a popular haircut in the Fifties, especially with Teddy Boys who used Brylcreem to keep the floppy quiff in place. But men who had done their national service stuck doggedly to a military 'short back and sides'. In the Sixties, young men grew their hair long and abandoned barbers in favour of the new uni-sex salons. These were given a wide berth by their dads who preferred men-only barber's shops, traditionally identified by a red-and-white striped pole over the door.

Robbie's sidecar

Lynda Taylor remembers a particularly dramatic first journey on the newly opened M6

The empty M6, a motorbike with a sidecar and my dog Robbie – so begins one of my earliest proper memories, aged seven years old in 1959.

My family and I had travelled from Leek in Staffordshire to take our first drive on what seemed then to be a very special road. Even at the age of seven I was aware that this was to be a memorable day.

I have learnt from historical reports that the first section of the M6, also known as the Preston Bypass, was opened in December 1958 by Harold Macmillan. It was eight and a quarter miles long with two lanes each way, more than enough for the traffic in those days. The road had been closed soon after its official opening due to frost damage, but was in use again early in 1959.

All I remember is that we went on a cold day in the early spring of that year, joining the motorway at its southern-most junction among the wonderful Staffordshire scenery, and headed north. I was too young to take any notice of the technical details of the road – for me, it was just an exciting day out at a time when family road travel was limited to special occasions. What has stayed very clearly in my memory is that the M6 was wide, long and almost deserted – a blessing as it later turned out. We saw only a couple of cars travelling the other way and nothing in view on our

No escape for Robbie on this occasion as Lynda tightly holds on to his lead.

side of the carriageway.

We were buzzing with excitement as we entered this new road, having looked at pictures in the paper and seen reports on our brand new television set (another novelty in those days). Dad drove at a moderate pace as we had the roof cover off our sidecar, even though it wasn't a warm day, to give me and mum a better view. I remember that I had on my best coat (for Sundays and outings), a woolly bobble hat and a matching scarf. I also had mittens hanging from my sleeves, attached to each other by the obligatory length of elastic through the sleeves of my

coat to prevent me from losing them. But I didn't really need them as I hugged my dog, Robbie, on my knee. He kept me lovely and snug, as he always did.

Robbie was a lively little West Island terrier, all white and fluffy. I don't know what the dog saw as we were travelling along, but suddenly he leapt off my knee, escaping my feeble grasp, bounded over my head and Mum's shoulder and landed on the motorway! Imagine the chaos that would cause today!

Dad quickly stopped at the side of the road and we all got out. Breaking all modern safety advice

adventure

Robbie behaving himself in the front of the sidecar. His M6 adventure prompted dad to cover-up the sidecar seats.

and rules, we stood right in the middle of the road calling to the dog to return to us. Fortunately, he was a reasonably obedient pet and eventually trotted back towards us unharmed.

Soon we were all laughing at Robbie's escapade, and he was unaware of any danger he could have put us in. I would like to be able to say that at this point we got out the flask and had a good old English cuppa and

a sandwich before setting out again, but I'm sure that would be me embellishing the event with memories of other days. I am certain that we used the opportunity to encourage the dog to do 'whatever he needed to do' while out of the sidecar though! No sense of rush or rules of the motorway on that day. After that, dad took the precaution of putting the roof cover on and we continued, now tightly packed

and sealed into our little box alongside dad's bike.

Robbie survived and remained with us until 1960; only a year on, but it seemed a long time to the small child I was then. We continued to have little escapades and he was my best friend. We were allowed to go off into the fields for walks and always had lovely adventures – but I don't remember him being allowed in that sidecar ever again!

The office party

BY: CAROLINE GAITSKELL

A sushi bar is not Martha's idea of festive fun

With a sense of foreboding about the evening ahead, Martha rifled through her wardrobe. What on earth was she going to wear? In previous years, the office Christmas do had been a sedate turkey dinner at a nearby restaurant; a brief interlude before returning to work in the afternoon.

Martha would have been happy to do the same again this year – one glass of wine and a joke from the cracker were enough frivolity for her these days. But this year had seen the arrival of a new director, much younger than old Mr Teal who'd recently retired from the family firm.

Young Mr Johnson was determined to drag the accountancy practice into the 21st century and Martha's job title of secretary had been updated to PA. She wondered how much longer she would be able to hold on to her trusty electric typewriter and found it sad that email was replacing telephone conversations.

"It's the future, Martha," Mr Johnson had told her on numerous occasions, trying to encourage her to embrace new technology.

His modernisation plans included the Christmas do which he'd chosen to hold after office hours at a popular sushi restaurant. The table wasn't booked until nine-thirty. At that time Martha was normally making a last cup of tea before watching the news and going to bed – not eating raw fish!

She felt she ought to show a proper sense of 'team spirit' by going to the meal, but definitely not staying for the disco afterwards.

Mr Johnson ('Please Martha, call me Tim') said that everyone could bring a guest, but Martha was not taking anyone. In the five years that she had been a widow she spent most Saturday nights alone. She had many friends, but at weekends they were at home with their husbands and families.

"You're definitely not bringing anyone, then?" Tim had asked her.

"You're definitely not bringing anyone, then?"

"No!" Martha hadn't meant to snap but she found questions about her personal life intrusive. She'd once told him that she and her husband had been keen ballroom dancers, but that she hadn't danced since George died, then had regretted giving Tim this glimpse of her apparently lonely life.

Now, in a calmer tone of voice, she asked: "Who are you bringing?"

"My wife. It will be nice for her to meet everyone and put names to faces."

Martha thought, 'Yes, I bet. No doubt he refers to me as the lonely old woman with no life outside the office'.

From her wardrobe, Martha selected a pair of well-cut black trousers and a sequinned blouse. The girls at work had been excitedly discussing their outfits all week but Martha felt a bit long in the tooth for anything too glamorous. At the back of the wardrobe she still had the pretty dresses and shoes she had worn when she had partnered George. Making a mental note to take them to a deserving charity shop, she completed her outfit with a pashmina.

When Martha stepped into the restaurant, she couldn't see anyone she recognised. The throng of people and the unfamiliar smell of exotic food distracted her and she was relieved to see Tim approaching.

"Hey, I'm so pleased you came. I was worried you might not turn up," he smiled.

"It's busy in here, isn't it?" Martha said. "Where is everyone?"

"At a table at the back of the restaurant. You've come on your own then?"

"As you can see," she replied, exasperated by his asking her yet again. "Is your wife with you?"

"She'll be joining us later – she had to babysit for a friend. I've brought my uncle along as my guest instead."

Tim led a reluctant Martha through the crowded tables to the one occupied by her colleagues. He found her an empty chair next to a man with greying hair.

Martha was astonished to find how late it was

"Uncle Edward, this is Martha, my PA," Tim introduced her.

"Delighted to meet you. Tim speaks highly of your work."

Martha blushed and looked round for Tim, but he was already heading for the bar. She sat down nervously but Edward quickly made her feel at ease. She was amazed at how much they had in common and they were soon engrossed in conversation.

Edward made her laugh with recollections of terrible Christmas cracker jokes. With his encouragement, she tried some sushi and was pleasantly surprised to find that she liked it. Maybe she would add it her next supermarket shopping list.

Martha was astonished to discover how late it was when bright flashing lights signified the start of the disco.

"I don't think much of this music," Edward shouted above the drumbeat. "This is the stuff Tim listens to. He likes everything modern – as you have probably discovered!"

"Perhaps, modern isn't all bad," Martha heard herself conceding. "It's the future, isn't it? And it's a lovely surprise when the future turns out not to be as awful as you expected. Tim suggested this place and it has been the best office Christmas party for years."

The music made conversation impossible so when Edward suggested they might attempt a waltz Martha surprised herself by readily agreeing.

As she joined him on the tiny dance floor, she caught sight of Tim watching them with a broad grin and suddenly Martha guessed why her new boss had asked so many personal questions…

Quick quiz

How many of these general knowledge questions can you answer? Turn the page upside down to see if you're right

1 Who said: "If you tell the truth, you don't have to remember anything"?

2 In the novel Little Women, what are the names of the four March sisters?

3 By what name is singer Arnold George Gerry Dorsey better known?

4 What does the naval acronym POSH stand for?

5 Which singer was famous for saying: "Thank you, thank you very much"?

6 Which famous sportsman is 'Oh Man I Bat' when the letters of his name are rearranged?

7 What is the name of the game that involves rolling five dice in various combinations?

8 Which actor played Norman Clegg for many years in Last of the Summer Wine and provided the voice for Wallace in the Wallace and Gromit films?

9 Which film, shot as a mixture of live action and animation, includes the song The Age Of Not Believing?

10 Which British wrestler was known by the nickname 'Big Daddy'?

11 Which vegetable is used in the layers of moussaka?

12 What is the main ingredient of 'Gnocci'?

13 Which tinned meat takes it name from 'spiced ham'?

14 Which star sign is represented by The Twins?

15 Which American comedian and actor provided the voice for Buzz Lightyear in the Toy Story films?

16 Name the two feuding families in Shakespeare's Romeo and Juliette.

17 What colour is the cross on the flag of Finland?

18 Which planet is the second from the sun and is named after the Roman Goddess of love and beauty?

PIC: REX FEATURES

1 Mark Twain, 2 Meg, Jo, Beth and Amy, 3 Engelbert Humperdinck, 4 Port Out, Starboard Home, 5 Elvis Presley, 6 Ian Botham, 7 Yahtzee, 8 Peter Sallis, 9 Bedknobs and Broomsticks, 10 Shirley Crabtree, 11 Aubergine, 12 Potato, 13 Spam, 14 Gemini, 15 Tim Allen, 16 Montague and Capulet, 17 Blue, 18 Venus

Let's go down the high street

Petrol stations arrived on the high street as the number of cars increased

PIC GETTY

"We never had it so good"

In the Fifties most people had an electric or gas cooker and a plug-in radio but only 30 per cent of homes had a washing machine. With full employment and increasing prosperity, that began to change and by the end of the decade many families had bought their first twin-tub washing machine, their first electric iron, maybe their first gramophone.

Many homes also had a TV set but these were more likely to be on hire from Rentaset or Radio Rentals as they were still very expensive to buy (a Ferguson 17in portable TV cost 58 guineas at a time when the average wage was around £10 a week).

Whether you were looking for carpet to replace the linoleum in your living room or a labour-saving vacuum cleaner, you could find everything under one roof in a department store. Londoners had Gamages, Whiteleys, Derry & Toms and many other long-gone names to choose from, but for people living elsewhere in the country the Co-op was likely to be their nearest one-stop shop. The Co-op supplied everything from milk to a funeral service and its customers collected stamps or tokens that were paid out as dividends twice a year – a useful way of saving money for those on a limited budget.

The place to go if you wanted to buy electrical gadgets or a gas cooker was the local gas and electricity board's showroom where you could also pay your utility bill or buy a bag of shillings to feed the slot meter.

Car showrooms began to appear on high streets as the number of privately owned cars rose steadily from 2m in 1948 to 3.5m in 1955. Hillman, Riley and Morris as well as Ford were all popular makes. Petrol pumps were often situated in the middle of town rather than on the outskirts and the tank was always filled by an attendant who would also check the oil and tyre pressures. There were fewer brands – Esso Extra and Shell were two of the best known and Shell had the catchiest jingle:

'We're going well, we're going Shell,
We're going well on Shell,
Shell, Shell!'

East End nursery

Lynne Whelon's time as a student nursery nurse in Sixties London had a lasting effect on her

" Just call the children inside please, Lynne." The Sister at the day nursery in Stratford, East London smiled kindly at me. It was 1967, I was 18 years old and it was my first day training as a nursery nurse. I think she could tell that I was a little bit nervous!

"Just clap your hands," she said cheerily, "and they'll all come running in."

So I stood just outside the door, which opened on to a concreted play area.

"Come and wash your hands children," I called loudly, "ready for lunch."

A small boy, aged about four, stood in front of me and smirked. None of the other children took the slightest notice of me and just carried on playing. The boy moved closer, spat on the ground and uttered two words, one of which was very rude, and made it quite clear that he did not really feel like coming in to wash his hands at that particular moment. I retreated back into the safety of the Toddler's Room and found Sister.

"They won't come in," I whimpered. "One of them just swore at me."

She raised her eyes heavenwards and proceeded to march outside.

"Get in here now!" she shouted.

Seconds later these terrifying children, aged from two to four years old, most of them only a quarter of my size, trotted obediently in and went to wash

Lynne had to learn how to exert her authority over the toddlers in her care. Once a year the children were treated to a trip to the seaside... for many youngsters it was their first time outside of London.

their hands. Many of them grinned cheekily at me on their way past.

"How did you manage that?" I asked Sister.

She shrugged her shoulders. "It'll come to you. Once you can assert your authority. Don't worry."

Of course she was right, although it did take some time! And so began two of the happiest years of my life.

I had been brought up mainly in the countryside, in Hampshire and Berkshire, before moving to Ilford in Essex. Living close to London was a huge culture shock for me. We moved there during the very bad winter of 1962/63

and the smog was so thick that we couldn't see where we were going at all!

At least I was in the right place to work with children when I left school. I had known for years it was what I wanted to do and so I was very excited when I was employed as a student nursery nurse in the London borough of Newham. For the next four years I worked in day nurseries, nursery schools and classes in primary schools in East London.

There were many children from poor homes in the day nursery and also some who suffered neglect and cruelty at home which we had to deal with as best we could. I remember

one family, three children, who often had no shoes on their feet when they came in on cold winter days. It may have been the Swinging Sixties in West London but this was a different world. Many other children I worked with lived in tower blocks which were all being built at that time. They had nowhere to play and the only fresh air they had was when they played outside at the nurseries. It must have been so hard for their parents.

The children themselves were very streetwise compared to any I had met before but also delightful. They were outgoing and full of mischief and had incredible imaginations. There was a lot of laughter.

Every year the taxi drivers in London would take us down to Southend so that the children could spend a day at the seaside. For many it was their first time out of London. They had never seen real sheep or cows. I think they were more excited about the animals we saw on the way than the sea at Southend! I told some of them about how we got milk from the cows. One little boy looked at me scornfully.

"That ain't true," he said. "Milk don't come from cows. It comes from the factory."

In the Sixties the ratios of staff to children were not quite what they are now. I remember one morning, in particular, when someone was off sick and I was working in the Baby Room on my own. Seventeen babies arrived before a nursery nurse finally came two hours later to help. That meant 17 nappies to be changed (towelling ones of course), all before 9am! The Matron, who was very scary, never thanked me, and in fact tore me off a strip because I hadn't polished the door handle!

Most of the parents and other Eastenders I met had a great sense of family and loyalty and were so kind even though they had nothing. Their wonderful sense of humour seemed to get them through the days and they rarely complained about their lot. The experience made me realise how easy my life had been compared to theirs and I have never forgotten it. It is now 47 years since that first lunchtime in the nursery, and I still look back on those days with great affection, and remember what characters I met and how much we laughed.

Recipe index

Yours Yearbook 2014

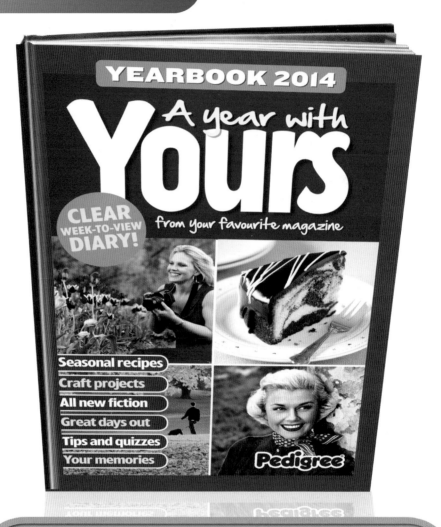

YEARBOOK 2014

A year with
Yours
from your favourite magazine

CLEAR
WEEK-TO-VIEW
DIARY!

Seasonal recipes
Craft projects
All new fiction
Great days out
Tips and quizzes
Your memories

Pedigree

Visit **Pedigreebooks.com** to find out more on this year's **Yours** Yearbook, scan with your mobile device to learn more.

Visit www.pedigreebooks.com

Pedigree Books, Beech Hill House, Walnut Gardens, Exeter EX4 4DH